TERF EVIL EYE EXPOSED

by
HENRI GAMACHE

Restored, Revised, and Edited by
CATHERINE YRONWODE
AND
DR. JEREMY WEISS

With Illustrations by
ABBÉ JEAN-ANTOINE DUBOIS
WILLIAM THOMAS PAVITT
CHARLES M. QUINLAN
GREGORY LEE WHITE
ET AL.

Lucky Mojo Library of Occult Classics
Lucky Mojo Curio Company
Forestville, California
2021

Terrors of the Evil Eye Exposed:
Protection Against Evil
by Henri Gamache [Anne Fleitman],
Restored, Revised, and Edited by catherine yronwode and Dr. Jeremy S. Weiss.

© 2021 catherine yronwode and Dr. Jeremy S. Weiss
LuckyMojo.com
TempleOfMiriam.com

All rights reserved under International and Pan-American Copyright Conventions. No part of this publication can be reproduced, stored in a retrieval system, or transmitted in any format by any means, electronic, mechanical, photocopying, recording, or otherwise, without the written permission of the copyright owner.

Text:
Henri Gamache [Anne Fleitman], catherine yronwode, Dr. Jeremy S. Weiss

Editor:
catherine yronwode

Cover:
Grey Townsend, Charles M. Quinlan

Typesetting:
catherine yronwode

Production:
nagasiva yronwode

Illustrations:
Charles M. Quinlan, Abbé Jean-Antoine Dubois, Gregory Lee White, William Thomas Pavitt, Grey Townsend, nagasiva yronwode, and Unknown Artists.

First Edition 2021

Published by
The Lucky Mojo Curio Company
6632 Covey Road
Forestville, California 95436
LuckyMojo.com

ISBN: 978-0-9997809-8-5

Printed in Canada.

TABLE OF CONTENTS

DEDICATION 4

ACKNOWLEDGEMENTS 4

WHO WROTE THIS BOOK? 5

A VALENTINE FOR ALAN DUNDES 6

PREFACE BY HENRI GAMACHE 8

   How It May Have Begun 9
   Where It Came From 10

1. A SURVEY OF THE EVIL EYE 11

   What People Call It 18
   Who Does It and
      How Do They Do It 20
   Who It Hurts and
      How to Help Them 21
   How It Is Prevented 22
   Why It Is Hidden Knowledge Today 23

2. A TAXONOMY OF THE EVIL EYE 24

   The Envious Eye 24
   The Eye of Unusual Appearance 26
   The Projective Evil Eye 27
   The Evil Eye's Effects on Children 30
   The Evil Eye's Effects on Mothers 30
   The Evil Eye's Effects on Women 31
   The Evil Eye's Effects on Men 31
   The Evil Eye's Effects on Animals 31
   The Evil Eye's Effects on Plants 31
   The Evil Eye's Effects on Eating 32
   When the Evil Eye is Powerless 33

3. PRECAUTIONS AGAINST THE EYE .. 36

4. AVERTING THE EVIL EYE 39

   Averting the Eye with Words 39
   Averting the Eye with Gestures 40
   Averting the Eye with Rituals 43
   Averting the Eye with Amulets 43
   The Colours Red and Blue 44
   Thread, String, and Cord Charms 46
   How to Make a Red String Bendel ... 47
   Eye Amulets 48
   Hand Amulets 50
   Bean, Seed, and Plant Curios 52
   Lemons to Avert the Evil Eye 54
   Rue to Repel the Evil Eye 55
   Shoes to Ward Off the Evil Eye 56
   Gendered Charms Against the Eye ... 57
   Mojo Hands to Ward Off Envy 59
   Spikes and Points to Pierce the Eye .. 60
   Miscellaneous Charms 61
   Protection in the Decorative Arts 64

5. DIAGNOSING THE EVIL EYE 78

6. CURING THE EVIL EYE 82

   Water or Holy Water as a Cure 83
   The "Showing" Cure for Children 84
   Burning the Evil Eye as a Cure 85
   Cutting the Eye as a Cure 88
   Transferring the Eye as a Cure 88
   Saliva as a Cure 89
   Salt as a Cure 91

7. IN CONCLUSION 93

8. ANNE FLEITMAN: THE WOMAN
   WHO WAS HENRI GAMACHE 94

BIBLIOGRAPHY 96

DEDICATION

This book is dedicated to the memory of Esther Paskin, a rationalist and science teacher who also knew about the *ayin hara*.

ACKNOWLEDGEMENTS

Our thanks go first and foremost to Anne Fleitman, who, as Henri Gamache, led me a merry chase for fifty years until the Library of Congress copyright records were digitized and she suddenly appeared in sight. We hope she would have been pleased with this Spiritualistic convocation between the living and the dead. All honour to her name.

Thanks to nagasiva yronwode, the stalwart cheerleader of so many projects that perpetuate and expand the study of folk magic, divination, and religion. He is the secret power-source behind the Lucky Mojo Library of Occult Classics and the Yronwode Institution for the Preservation and Popularization of Indigenous Ethnomagicology — YIPPIE.

Thanks to Grey Townsend, our graphic designer, for cleaning up and making new separations for the cover of this book, and also for jamming his way through 87 illustrations, two book covers, one tattered flyer, and a half-page catalogue ad as well. Thank you, Grey!

Thanks to the authors whose works we have consulted: Frederick Elworthy, Joshua Trachtenberg, Alan Dundes, Isaac Jack Levy, and Rosemary Levy Zumwalt; and thanks to the artists: Abbé Dubois, the uncredited Wills cigarette card illustrator (whom i am crediting as William Thomas Pavitt), and Gregory Lee White, my amuletic co-author.

Thanks to Leslie Lowell, Heidi Simpson, Eileen Edler, Ernie Medeiros, Nicole Carevich, Althea Anderson, Jenne Nelson, Elvyra Curcuruto-Love, Summer Burkes, Sunny Santos, and Colleen Buchanan, who kept the wheels of prayer and commerce turning at Lucky Mojo while we were writing.

Thanks to Roi Geyari for help with Hebrew translations and transliterations; to Jennifer Tiffany Johnson for sharing her family's folklore; and to the ConjureMan, our radio podcast co-host on the Lucky Mojo Hoodoo Rootwork Hour, for vetting some of the Arabic lore.

And thanks to our patient and discerning proofreaders, Summer Burkes and Fred Burke.

WHO WROTE THIS BOOK?

"Terrors of the Evil Eye Exposed" (also known as *"Protection Against Evil"*) was a popular American magical grimoire by Henri Gamache that remained continually in print from 1946 through 2006. Marketed and sold via a nationwide network of African-American conjure shops and hoodoo drugstores, it kept alive ancient African traditions about the evil eye, presented Jewish evil eye customs through the Christian lens of the Old Testament, and delved into the seemingly exotic, yet very familiar, evil eye beliefs of India and Pakistan.

The author chose these regions as exemplars of the depth and breadth of evil eye customs in specific geographic areas, and in page after well-researched page, prescribed preventions, protections, and cures for the evil eye to generations of root doctors and home practitioners, none of whom knew that Henri Gamache, also the author of *"The Master Book of Candle Burning,"* was actually a woman named Anne Fleitman.

However, Anne Fleitman was the author of only about about half of the book you now hold in your hands. As originally printed, it was a square-bound 96 pager, just like this edition, but the page layout was such that when it was retypeset, the words filled only one-half of our present book format. The writing was excellent and there was nothing wrong with *"Terrors of the Evil Eye Exposed"* — it was just too short!

Loving the book as much as we did, we — catherine yronwode and Dr. Jeremy Weiss — chose to expand it to give readers an even wider world survey of evil eye beliefs, customs, and remedies. To Fleitman's solid core of research on Africa and India, we have added evil eye charms and talismans of the Middle East, North America, and Europe. In addition, we have broken Fleitman's continuous narrative into new chapters, then re-ordered the chapters, added distinct sub-sections, and gave the specific charms and remedies short, bold-face titles to make them easier to locate.

By using the resources of catherine's Lucky W Amulet Archive — online since 1994 and now in its new home at AmuletArchive.org — we have greatly expanded the section on warding off the evil eye with apotropaic charms, but for more on the subject of magical amulets of all kinds, we suggest that you search out the companion volume to this book:

"How to Use Amulets, Charms, and Talismans in the Hoodoo and Conjure Tradition" by catherine yronwode and Gregory Lee White.

A VALENTINE FOR ALAN DUNDES

Many books have been written about the evil eye. The classic 19th century text is *"The Evil Eye: The Origins and Practices of Superstition"* by Frederick Thomas Elworthy, but the most thought-provoking academic essay on the psychology and world distribution of evil eye belief is *"Wet and Dry: The Evil Eye"* by Professor Alan Dundes (1934-2005). This article can be found in two of his books, *"Interpreting Folklore"* and *"The Evil Eye: A Casebook,"* the latter a collection of scholarly writings assembled as a text for his folklore students at th University of California.

Dundes theorized that the evil or envious eye is based upon underlying beliefs about water equating to life and dryness equating to death. He posited that the true "evil" done by the evil eye is that it causes living beings to "dry up" — notably babies, milking animals, young fruit trees, nursing mothers, and male genitals. The eye brings on sudden vomiting or diarrhœa in children, dries up the milk of women or livestock, withers fruit on orchard trees, and causes loss of potency in men. In short, the envious eye "dries up liquids," according to Dundes — which he contended demonstrates its Middle Eastern desert origins.

Once you understand his premise, the entire array of regional evil eye beliefs falls into logical patterns. Blue objects protect because water is blue. Red objects protect because blood is red. Saliva is wet, semen is wet, holy water is wet, and female genitalia are wet. The Lemon is an eye, the egg is an eye, Almonds are eyes, and Aspand is an eye. Nails and pins can pierce an evil eye, and heat can explode it, causing it to die before it can drain the liquid life out of its victims.

As Dundes pointed out, evil eye belief spread out in a radiating ring from the ancient Middle East. It is found among Jews, Muslims, Zoroastrians, and Christians. It reaches across Europe, the Balkans, Greece, and Turkey, to the Levant, Eurasia, and onward to India and the Himalayas. In the South it runs from the Mediterranean shores well down into Central and South Africa. The era of colonization and slavery carried it into Latin America, North America, Australia, and New Zealand. It is now found almost everywhere.

But what is it? What is the danger of the whammy, the squint eye, the *ojo malo*? That, dear friend, you are about to find out!

And before we begin, let us acknowledge our debt to Alan Dundes for his many books on folklore, and especially for his exegesis on the evil eye.

Cover of a four-page occult book catalogue featuring the first edition of *"Terrors of the Evil Eye Exposed;"* art by Charles M. Quinlan, 1946; all the titles advertised were printed by Joe Kay.

PREFACE BY HENRI GAMACHE

This book may come as a distinct shock to many people. To some, the facts stated may seem fantastic and incredible. Many will not be able to reconcile these facts with the present state of science ... with the splitting of the atom and with advances in many other lines of endeavour. Yet the fact still remains that the power behind witchcraft guides the daily activities of more than half the people of this world, and although witchcraft may seem to have outlived its usefulness in a modern world, it was at one time an honourable calling and to it many of our modern sciences owe a debt.

Witchcraft in the United States did not go out with the Salem witches. It still persists, not alone in the hills of Kentucky and Tennessee, the marsh-lands of the Gulf States, and in other isolated areas, but in many respectable towns and in our very largest cities. To one who has made a study of the survival of ancient beliefs within contemporary folkloric customs, it seems incredible that so few people know of the existence of witchcraft in our day or, recognizing its existence, fail to consider its importance to so many people. If one is inclined to doubt the prevalency of such beliefs in America and even to question the great number of beliefs and customs which have been enumerated in this present volume, the writer refers you to *"Witches Still Live"* by Theda Kenyon, in which it is stated that in Kentucky alone more than 3,954 different superstitions have been tabulated.

It must not be thought for a moment that the customs which are about to be described belong only to some distant generation, to the Middle Ages, or to geographically remote civilizations. These customs are still followed by people in our own generation, in our own small towns and villages, and in our own great cities. The belief in the power of the evil eye is as alive today as it was four thousand years ago.

Such a generally accepted belief cannot be exterminated through mockery or prohibition. This treatise, by open-minded inquiry and a straightforward presentation of facts, is an attempt to give the reader some idea of the widespread prevalence of the belief in the dangers of the evil eye, to describe preventive customs that avert it and attested cures that are said to end its damage, and to impregnate one thought in the mind of the reader: the futility of trying to circumvent fear.

HOW IT MAY HAVE BEGUN

Today we regard with respect a person who can look you straight in the eye when he talks to you. It is a form of sincerity; it inspires belief. This has not always been true, however, for in times gone by, no peasant dared to look upon his lord, no slave upon his master, and no subject upon his king. He must talk to his superiors only if he averted his eyes.

This could, of course, be an off-shoot of the premise that there is some inherent evil which lurks in the eyes, but from my own studies, I am not inclined to believe that people feel there is evil in the eyes. Rather, I think that the reason for forbidding a person of low status to gaze directly into the eyes of one of high status is based upon the thought behind the glance — the fear of an envious thought.

Let us suppose that a man owns a cow and a neighbour comes to look at it. He wishes that he had such a fine cow and he looks longingly at it and is envious of his neighbour for having such a fine beast.

The man sees the envious look in his neighbour's eyes and says to himself, "I must be careful or my neighbour will steal my cow."

The neighbour comes several times and each time the man sees the envy in his neighbour's eyes as he looks upon the cow. Then one day the cow falls sick — for no apparent reason — and it dies. Immediately the erstwhile owner of the cow accuses his neighbour of having "put the eye" upon the cow to cause its death.

Envy, greed, and covetousness are considered immoral in his culture. Thereafter word spreads and people avoid the neighbour, for they fear he may "put the eye" upon them. The neighbour finds himself an outcast; unwanted, unloved. He becomes incensed; he takes to brooding and thinks up ways of getting even, and so he deliberately goes out of his way to fix his piercing and malevolent gaze upon all whom he meets.

Now let us see what results. In the natural course of events accidents happen: A child or a beast of the household becomes sick; a man breaks his leg; a woman has a miscarriage. Every time something of the sort happens, the sufferers attribute it to one cause, namely "the eye" of their neighbour. In time, his gaze of envy is seen as an eye of evil.

This, it seems to me, is a common pattern which exists throughout literature, legend, and tradition — and it can form a rationalist's theory of the origin of the evil eye.

WHERE IT CAME FROM

For a number of years the subject of the evil eye has been of great interest to writers, in part because the terrors of the evil eye have overcome people of every nationality, of every religion, of every degree of education, of every tint of skin, and of every walk of life. There is hardly a week which passes in which we have not noted this influence at work or in the press. It is unnoticed by most people simply because they have failed to recognise it. But because it is everywhere, two questions arise:

How far back in human history did it begin?

Where in the world did it first originate?

FROM FOLKLORE TO THE WRITTEN WORD

How far back into antiquity this influence goes no one rightly knows, but that it is an outgrowth of early human philosophies based upon nature cults, traditions of medical and magical healing, and the belief in witchcraft or curses is definitely known ... and these are as old as humanity itself.

The most prominent symbols associated with the evil eye belief are the eye and the hand, important symbols of protection against the eye.

We certainly find hand-prints as images dating back to prehistoric cave art. But were these hands meant to be symbols of protection against the evil eye — or did they have a different meaning to the cave artists? Eye-art is almost as old as hand-art, but again we face the impossibility of assigning meaning to prehistoric art.

Only when descriptions of magical beliefs and ritual activities enter written documents can their date be assessed — but the date at which a belief, custom, or spiritual prescription first enters the world of documentable evidence is not always the date of its origin. Every culture on Earth adopted the practice of writing at a different time, and it cannot be presumed that if we know the date of a given culture's first written documents we will be able to decipher their language, or that their beliefs did not long pre-date their invention or adoption of writing.

Scholarly assertions and assumptions aside, all we can do is take as a certainty that a fully developed understanding of the evil eye belief system is noted in many ancient documents, and that images that seem to relate to the evil eye have a previous history stretching far back into mankind's misty past, in Africa and the Middle East.

1. A SURVEY OF THE EVIL EYE

Among many cultures there is a symbolism involved in magical rites. Certain actions, certain articles of ritual, and certain procedures can be interpreted symbolically. This is true of priestly Egyptian magic, tribal rituals of Africa, the religious magic of the Isrælites, Zoroastrians, Christians, Muslims, and Hindus; and the domestic folklore of the American South, the West Indies, the Mediterranean, and the Ægean.

This symbolism, more often than not, had a deep religious significance. It was not merely superstition. It may have been steeped in tradition, legend, and folklore, but by the symbolism involved it maintained a certain dignity, recognized an omnipotent power, and became a satisfying performance to those who participated in it.

THE EVIL EYE IN THE ANCIENT MIDDLE EAST

The ancient Mesopotamian region gave rise to the Sumerian, Assyrian, Akkadian, and Babylonian civilizations. Of these, the Sumerian culture was the earliest, originating between the Tigris and Euphrates rivers around 4000 BCE. Among the many artifacts found in Sumerian ruins are written spells against the evil eye, one of which mentions the apotropaic blue stone, lapis lazuli. Bloodshot eyes are also associated with the evil eye in ancient Sumer, in a spelltext that reads, *"The eye [is] a red snake, the eye of the man [is] a red snake, the eye of the evil man is a red snake."* The evil red snake-eye in this text is said to bring drought, loss of crops, loss of strength, and loss of livestock.

In the poem that describes the descent of the goddess Inanna into the underworld, the evil eye sent against her is "the eye of death," essentially what Americans call the whammy: *"They looked at her — it was the eye of death. They spoke to her — it was the speech of illness. They shouted at her — it was the shout of damnation. The afflicted woman became a corpse. The corpse was hung on a hook."* Inanna escaped this situation and later killed her unfaithful husband Dumuzi with her own "eye of death."

Other Sumerian gods and goddesses also cast the evil eye or *igi hul*, among them Enlil, Enki, and Ninisina. Lord Enlil could even set his evil eye to roam about on its own to wreak devastation on the land. This was called *igi nigin* ("the eye goes around") and sounds like J. R. R. Tolkien's later fictional concept of the Eye of Sauron in *"The Lord of the Rings."*

THE EVIL EYE IN ANCIENT EGYPT

Ancient Egyptians believed evil-doers could cast misfortune upon their victims by means of an intentional gaze. They also held that the image of an eye was a powerful charm to ward off evil, reflecting it back to the one who sent it. The eye of the god Horus, known as the wadjet, wedjat, or udjat, was used as a symbol of protection and good health, made into amulets to be worn on the person. It still finds popularity today as a wall-hanging, personal charm, or tattoo. Its colour is quite often blue.

THE EVIL EYE IN AFRICA

Africa is rich in material on the subject of the evil eye, but the original sources of African folklore are difficult to pinpoint, because written language did not develop in central Africa until relatively recently.

It is logical to theorize that indigenous belief in the evil eye originated in central Africa from a prehistoric source. It is also logical to theorize that the belief arose in ancient Egypt and spread South, or that it was carried to Egypt from the Middle East by the Isrælite slaves, from whence it made its way into the interior of Africa and dispersed over the entire continent.

Another theory holds that during the previous millennium, the incursions of Iberian, Mediterranean, and North African Muslim slave traders into continental Africa may have spread a second or third wave of evil eye beliefs into territories they controlled. Many contemporary Africans are Muslims, and their evil eye practices have been influenced by Arab sources.

Africans often differentiate between sending the evil eye intentionally and not doing so purposefully. In the first case the sender is definitely responsible; in the second he may be excused. However, this excusal does not eliminate the possibility that evil intentions may remain in the man who harbours them — even though he himself may not be conscious of it.

Among the Herero Bantus of Southern Africa, it is believed that suppressed anger and resentment are the cause of the evil eye. For example, a sick person is thought to resent the good health that another enjoys and it is therefore believed that the glance of a sick person has the power to injure the soul of another and to consume its power.

In modern times, it is quite common to learn of African immigrants to America who have fallen ill due to the jealousy of family members they left behind in their homelands. This is sometimes called "envy from across the sea."

THE EVIL EYE IN ANCIENT PERSIA

The Achæmenid Persian Empire was ruled by Zoroastrians who believed in the evil eye and used Aspand to ward it off. Persia fell to the Greeks, then to the Byzantine Romans, and finally to the Muslim Arabs, who adopted the Zoroastrian rituals against the evil eye.

THE EVIL EYE IN ANCIENT GREECE AND ROME

The evil eye was feared in Greece and it also affected the Romans, for in the poetry of Virgil we find the following verse spoken by a shepherd: *"Nescio quis teneros oculus mihi fascinat agnos."* (*"I don't know what evil eye bewitches my lambs."*)

In imperial Rome, when a conqueror returned to march in triumph, there was always a statue of the phallic god Fascinus on display, to capture the eyes of the envious and preserve the warrior from the malignant gaze of onlookers. In bas-reliefs, the victory of Fascinus over the evil eye was represented by the winged penis ejaculating onto a disembodied eye.

THE EVIL EYE IN THE JEWISH BIBLE

We can find references to the evil eye in Deuteronomy, the Fifth Book of Moses, written in the 7th century BCE. From this we can deduce that the evil eye was well known to the Jews whom Moses led out of Egypt.

The Book of Proverbs, ascribed to King Solomon, also references the evil eye. As it bears signs of literary influence from earlier Egyptian wisdom collections, it may have been adopted by Jews enslaved in Egypt.

Even the minor prophet Amos mentions the use of the eye for evil.

- Deuteronomy 15:9: *"Beware that there be not a thought in thy wicked heart, saying, the seventh year, the year of release, is at hand; and thine eye be evil against thy poor brother…"*
- Proverbs 10:10: *"He that winketh with the eye causeth sorrow."*
- Proverbs 23:6: *"Eat thou not the bread of him that hath an evil eye, neither desire thou his dainty meats."*
- Proverbs 28:22: *"A man with an evil eye hastens after riches, and does not consider that poverty will come upon him."*
- Amos 9:4,10: *"And though they go into captivity before their enemies, thence will I command the sword, and it shall slay them: and I will set mine eyes upon them for evil, and not for good."*

THE EVIL EYE AMONG MODERN JEWS
Jews recognize three ways to ward off, combat, or cure the evil eye.

- **An apotropaic amulet:** A *kamea* ("amulet;" the plural is *kameot*) may be worn, carried, or placed in a location to turn away the eye.
- **A ritual of protection:** A *ma'aseh* ("deed or action;" the plural is *ma'asim*) may be performed to ward off the eye.
- **A magical remedy:** A *segula* ("remedy, treasure, talisman;" the plural is *segulot*) can be employed to cure the evil eye.

A great deal of attention is paid by Jews to protecting babies from *ayin hara*, the evil eye. Red threads and other charms, such as the eye-in-hand, hamsa hand, and fish charms, may be employed for this purpose.

In keeping with Professor Dundes' theory that the evil eye symbolizes a loss of fluids, it is interesting to note that Jews hold that fishes are immune to *ayin hara* "because they are covered with water." Furthermore, the descendants of a man named Yosef Tzaddik (literally Joseph the Righteous, but also a pun on the Hebrew letter Tzaddi or Fish-Hook) are immune to the evil eye because he was never jealous, his name relates to fishes, and he was a descendant of the Biblical Joseph, son of Jacob, who, along with Jacob's granddaughter Serah Bat Asher, was also immune to the evil eye.

Envy of fertility is found in Midrashic interpretations of the Bible, where it is suggested that Abraham's infertile wife Sarah gave his concubine Hagar a miscarriage with her evil eye. Early Jewish belief in the evil eye resulted in community safeguards to prevent such events. For instance, rather than taking a census and thus opening some people up to jealous eyes because they had large families, it was the custom for each person to pay a shekel (a small coin) to the census taker and let the coins be counted rather than peoples' names, to avoid envy. The best month for taking such a coin-census was said to be in the month which is associated with the zodiacal sign of Pisces (*Dagim*, The Fishes), because "fishes are immune to *ayin hara*."

In the Talmuud *(Bava Metzia 107b)* the sage Rav noted that "out of 100 people buried a graveyard, 99 died because of *ayin hara*," but although some modern Jews downplay *ayin hara* as "superstition," they still explain it theologically, saying, "When someone is jealous, he makes a complaint that is heard by God, and if the person who is being complained against is proud or ungenerous, then God judges him and lowers him."

THE EVIL EYE IN INDIA

The Hindus, even in ancient times, were aware of the evil eye. They called it *drishti*, which means "focussed gaze." *Drishti* may refer to single-pointed attention in meditation, but in common speech, it is the same as a "gaze" of Scotland or *ayin hara* among the Jews. There are several Hindu religious books which treat of *drishti* and other magical arts. Chief among them is the *"Atharva-Veda"* or *"Fourth Veda,"* as it is popularly known. This is a collection of formulæ to avert the consequences of mistakes or mishaps of various kinds. The recitation of this Veda is said to confer longevity, to cure diseases, to obtain success in love or gaming, to effect the ruin of enemies, and to secure the reciter's prosperity.

Although to most minds the term evil eye means but one thing, among the Hindus, it is a general term that defies complete, accurate analysis, for it includes evil in many different forms. For this reason, the Hindus have a most prolific and complex literature on the subject of the evil eye.

THE EVIL EYE IN CHRISTIAN EUROPE

In the Book of Mark 7:21-22, we see that the early Christians, who adhered to many Jewish customs, believed in the evil eye, for when Jesus lectured about defilement, he mentioned it:

"For from within, out of the heart of men, proceed evil thoughts, adulteries, fornications, murders, thefts, covetousness, wickedness, deceit, lasciviousness, an evil eye, blasphemy, pride, foolishness."

When Christianity took hold in Rome, the evil eye belief was already there, but as Christian converts spread out from Rome and European pagans were in turn converted to Catholicism, the idea moved Northward until, during the fifteenth century, it reached its peak in Europe.

The beliefs which surround the evil eye are now common everywhere in Europe, but more strongly expressed in areas closer to the Levant and North Africa, and in regions where Jewish people were permitted to settle. French peasants hastily draw their children away from a stranger or ill-looking person for fear his glance will cast a spell over the little ones. The same is true in Italy, Bulgaria, Romania, Portugal, Spain, and Greece.

In Europe, as in every other region, it is not only the poor, the ignorant, or the uneducated who sense the evil and envious eyes which surround them. There are many European people in the highest places who consciously work to circumvent these influences.

THE EVIL EYE IN ISLAM

The religion of Islam originated in the 7th century CE in Arabia. It sprang from Semitic roots and thus bears some cultural similarities to Judaism. Within a few centuries it spread across North Africa, the Levant, the Middle East, Eurasia, Eastern Europe, and South Asia. With it went characteristic Middle Eastern beliefs and practices. Evil eye lore is so embedded in Arab culture that four forms of it are recognized:

- **Ayn:** The eye from someone who knows and may even love you, and had no intention of harming you, but feels envy nonetheless.
- **Hasad:** The evil eye of envy from someone who dislikes you and wants what you have.
- **Nafs:** The evil eye of self-admiration, ego, and narcissism which you can put upon yourself.
- **Nathara:** The evil eye which is cast upon human beings by djinns or discarnate spirits of the desert.

Among Muslims, the evil eye is typically said to be transmitted in the form of praise which conceals envy, bringing on illness in children. However, it can be prevented if the protective Arabic phrase *"Masha Allah"* ("With the will of Allah" or "God willed it") is spoken, indicating that the child's beauty or cleverness is not something to envy, because God caused it to be so, and God's will is not to be questioned.

In Sahih Muslim, Book 26, Hadith #5427, the Prophet Muhammad said, *"The influence of an evil eye is a fact; if anything would precede the destiny it would be the influence of an evil eye, and when you are asked to take a bath (as a cure) from the influence of an evil eye, you should take the bath."* Many people read the last three chapters of the Quran (Sura Ikhlas, Sura Al-Falaq and Sura Al-Nas) to ward off the evil eye, carry written talismans called *"tawiz,"* or wear an called the hamsa hand or hand of Fatima, after Fatima al-Zahra, the daughter of the Prophet.

In Islamic cultures, the influence of the evil eye can be so close to other evil influences that they overlap and it is difficult to distinguish one evil from another. For instance, a Muslim may speak both of the "evil eye" and the "evil foot" as being influenced by an "unfavourable star," in the astrological sense, and the custom of washing the feet is a common precaution against both forms of evil.

THE EVIL EYE ON FAR-FLUNG CONTINENTS

The manner in which the surging power of the evil eye covered Africa and Europe does not account for the manner in which it sprang up in many other parts of the world. It cannot be definitely stated that the early Isrælites adopted the subject of the evil eye from the Egyptians, nor can it be said that the Hindus learned it through ancient trade with Semitic people.

Some of the rituals of Africa are similar to those of islanders of the South Pacific or of the Inuit. One wonders why this is so. Certainly we must go beyond mere chance contact; we cannot believe that such widely spread beliefs come originally from a single source. It must be an instinctive urge or fear arising within man himself. It must be a fear that is primeval as the instinct of self preservation.

We know that by the time of the founding of Islam in the 7th century CE, the belief was embedded in many cultures and that they spread it widely. We know that Spanish, Portuguese, and French colonists carried the belief with them to Latin America as early as the 1500s. And we know that these were followed into the Western Hemisphere by Jewish, Sicilian, Greek, Turkish, Syrian, Lebanese, Indian, Pakistani, and Romani immigrants who brought their evil eye charms and rituals with them.

Strangely enough, however, a pattern of similarity seems to run all through the subject regardless where it may be found. The amulets to counteract the evil eye that come from India resemble those of faraway South America or of the native North Americans. Study of the culture of these peoples shows that the evil eye was accepted by them as a fact of life. So how can we account for the origin of evil eye belief on the Islands of the South Pacific, in Australia, among the Inuit, among the native North Americans, among the Mayans of Mexico, and the Incas of South America?

Because the beliefs, and, more importantly, the methods employed to overcome the influence of the evil eye, are so close among different cultures, it seems that either one must have borrowed from another or that they all derive from an even more ancient common source to which each culture had access.

To many scholars, the only rational explanation that we can have for such a phenomena is that there is some natural instinct deep within man which causes him to recognize the influence of the envious eye.

WHAT PEOPLE CALL IT

Regional names for the evil eye are diverse and those that originate in languages that employ non-Latin alphabets have many variant spellings.

Abelske Oko: Czech
Atchkov Tal: Armenian
Ayin Hara: Hebrew
Ayn Hasad: Arabic
Begi Gaiztoa: Basque
Boeser Blick: German
Bouda: Ethiopian
Boze Oog: Dutch
Bur Akha: Punjabi
Buree Najar: Hindi
Cattivu Ochju: Corsican
Char Atchk: Armenian
Cheshmeh Hasood: Persian
Cheshmeh Nazar: Persian
Deochi: Romanian
Diavoliko Mati: Greek
Double Whammy: English
Drishti: Kannada
Drishti Dosha: Sanskrit
Droch Ahuil: Irish, Scottish
Durnoy Glaz: Russian
Dyavolsko Oko: Bulgarian
Goz Deymesi: Azerbaijani
Erbet Goez: Turmen
Evil Eye: English
Gonosz Szem: Hungarian
Ilaaco: Somali
Jakhendar: Romani
Jashi: Japanese
Jettatura: Sicilian
Jinx: English
Kannu Veykkuka: Malayam

Kannuru: Tamil
Kan Padudhal: Tamil
Kem Goez: Turkish
Maka Pilau: Hawaiian
Mal de Ojo: Spanish
Mal de Ollo: Gallician
Mal D'ull: Catalan
Maljo (Mal Yeaux): Trinidadian
Malocchio: Italian
Malu Ochju: Corsican
Mau Olhado: Portuguese
Mauvais Oeil: French
Nazar: Turkish
Nazar Lagna: Urdu, Hindi
Oculus Malus: Latin
Olho Gordo: Portuguese
Onda Ogat: Swedish
Ondt Oje: Danish
Paha Silmä: Finnish
Squint Eye: English
Stink Eye: English
Syni Keq: Albanian
Syri I Keq: Albanian
Szemmelveres: Hungarian
Thiat: Wolof, Senegalese
Urokljivo Oko: Serbian
Whammy: English
Xie Yan: Chinese
Yomon Ko'z: Uzbek
Zle Oko: Ukrainian
Zlo Oko: Bosnian, Croatian
Zulim Koez: Kazakh

Cover art cut-and-pasted from the original by Charles M. Quinlan for the 1969 and later editions, retitled *"Protection Against Evil."*

WHO DOES IT AND HOW THEY DO IT

PERPETRATORS OF THE EVIL EYE

- Envious people
- Those who praise children
- Those who are covetous
- Childless women
- Women who were unable to nurse their children
- Men who have no son and envy those who do
- Women who have miscarried
- People who have no children
- Orphans who have lost their parents
- Poor people
- Hungry or thirsty people
- Hungry or thirsty animals
- Thirsty plants
- Blue-eyed people who are uncommon among brown-eyed people
- Cross-eyed and wall-eyed people
- Squint-eyed people
- People born with the propensity to inadvertently project the eye

HOW THE EVIL EYE IS TRANSMITTED

- Overlooking or gazing too long upon a coveted item
- Gazing with covetousness upon a farm animal or pet
- Looking upon a child with jealousy because it is another's
- Praising without touching to void the damage
- Praising without spitting or pretending to spit to void the damage
- Praising without saying *"kein ayin hara"* to void the damage
- Praising without saying *"Masha Allah"* to void the damage
- Asking God why another person has something you do not have
- Wishing ill upon those who have more than you have
- Having a natural evil eye and not looking down to shield people
- Projection from the eye through an intentionally hard gaze
- Deliberately putting the eye on someone or something
- Deliberately giving someone the whammy or the squint eye

WHO IT HURTS AND HOW TO HELP THEM

VICTIMS OF THE EVIL EYE (AND THEIR SYMPTOMS)

- Nursing infants (they sicken, cry, vomit, and have diarrhœa)
- Breastfeeding mothers (their milk dries up)
- Young children (they vomit, sweat, or become listless)
- Milk cows and milk goats (their milk dries up)
- Fruit trees (they wither and die or they do not bear fruit)
- Fathers and sons (one of them will sicken or die)
- Mothers and daughters (one of them will sicken or die)
- Daughters (they are unlucky in love, unmarriageable, or childless)
- Adult men (they become impotent or sterile)

CURES FOR THE EVIL EYE

- Olive oil dripped into water with prayer
- Wax dripped into water with prayer
- Coals or burnt matches dropped into water; drinking the coal-water
- Piercing or cutting the evil eye
- Piercing a Lemon with iron nails
- Transfer of the evil eye to the ground in the form of a liquid
- Passing a whole raw egg over the face, then breaking it
- Breaking an egg in a dark, shadowed place, unseen
- Breaking an egg and drawing a cross on the victim's forehead
- Throwing an egg into the bushes or against a tree (if tree is victim)
- Placing a broken egg in a dish beneath the victim's bed
- Victim drinks three sips of holy water
- Victim is bathed in holy water
- Victim or victim's guardian spits at the perpetrator three times
- Victim's guardian licks or kisses the victim
- Victim's guardian pretends to spit at the perpetrator
- Water or spittle from perpetrator is passed to mouth of victim
- Collection of spittle from group; victim drinks it in holy water
- Fumigation with Aspand popped on charcoal and recitation of a spell
- Fumigation with Clove buds popped on charoal
- Burning efficacious items such as broom straws

HOW IT IS PREVENTED

APOTROPAIC GESTURES, PHRASES, AND CHARMS

- Refusal to accept praise on behalf of child
- Putting a spot of soot or dirt on the child so it will not look pretty
- Spitting on, licking, or kissing the child
- Fig, Descendents of Joseph, or Clasped Thumbs hand gesture
- Saying the verse of the descendants of Joseph
- Mano Fica or Thumb in Fist hand gesture, amulets, or jewelry
- Mano Cornuto or Horned Hand gesture, amulets, or jewelry
- Saying *"kein ayin hara"* or *"Masha Allah"*
- Asking the perpetrator to say *"kein ayin hara"* or *"Masha Allah"*
- Keeping travel and wedding plans secret
- Covering the food at table with a cloth before serving
- Cimaruta amulets or jewelry
- All-Seeing eye amulets or jewelry
- Utchat or Wadjet eye amulets or jewelry
- Dzi beads
- Blue glass eye disks / Nazar Boncugu / Nazar Boncuk / Nazar Bonjuk
- Blue paint, blue water, blue soap, blue bottles, and blue stone beads
- Cord charms that decay and release a blue bead
- Eye-agate amulets or jewelry; the Eye of Buddha
- *Ojo de Venado* or Deer's Eye seeds
- Jumbie Beans
- Cat's-eye shells
- Eye-in-hand amulets
- Hand of Power and Powerful Hand / Mano Poderosa images
- Hamsa hand / Hamesh hand / Hand of Fatima / Hand of Miriam
- Fish-shaped amulets and jewelry, the zodiac sign of Pisces
- Mirrors, mirror embroidery, and mirror charms
- Red threads or red cords, with or without blue beads
- Red coral horns, hands, and twigs
- Girdle or Buckle of Isis amulets
- Horseshoe and horseshoe nail; nail from the left-foot shoe of a man
- Crescent-shaped or tusk-shaped amulets
- Wolf, Bear, or Elephant hair

WHY IT IS HIDDEN KNOWLEDGE TODAY

Of all the forms of witchcraft, perhaps the one which holds the greatest terror for those susceptible to its influence is the evil eye.

One reason for this is that although the eye is the conductor of the evil influence to the victim, the actual evil arises from the disposition of the person who casts the eye. The one who gives the eye is incensed with envy, and we all know that an angry person can be dangerous.

There is a predisposition on the part of those who have once been bewitched to fear persons and things with which they come in daily contact. Were it not for this learned fear, the evil eye would hold far fewer terrors for the common man. However, many people having felt the influence of the eye, it has become an almost taboo topic among certain populations.

In these places, if you were to hear someone mention the subject and to politely inquire as to just what was meant by the term "evil eye," or to ask how you can tell if someone "has the evil eye," or "was given the evil eye," you might get one of these common reactions:

- **A Fear of the Eye:** The individual might become alarmed and retire at the first opportunity. This is especially true of a person from a culture with a strong evil eye belief. His reasoning might be that those who ask such questions are most prone to giving the evil eye.

- **A Culture Barrier:** The individual might attempt to tell how the evil eye operates within his culture, but he would be vague in his description or would be so conscious of the difficulty of explaining the eye's specialized terminology to an "outsider" that he would soon fall silent.

- **A Stone Wall:** The individual might say, "I just know it, that's all," and you would not be able to get another shred of evidence as to what it is or what it means. His reasoning might be that those who ask such foolish questions are skeptics, and he has no time for arguments.

This book, therefore, has two aims: first, to help "outsiders" understand the evil eye, and second — and most importantly — to help those of us familiar with the evil eye to learn more about it, so that we may better avert its influence, protect our loved ones, and cure afflictions by the eye.

2. A TAXONOMY OF THE EYE

THE ENVIOUS EYE

The concept of envy is so central to the evil eye that terms like the eye of envy and the invidious eye are frequently used to describe it.

THE EYE OF JEALOUS DESIRE

If one becomes sick to the stomach or suffers nausea, vomiting, or abdominal distension after eating, it is often thought to have been caused by an evil-eyed person intruding during a meal. The glutton is also held at a distance because he covets food even when he has it, and a hungry man may enviously inflict the evil eye on those who are eating.

The evil eye may be cast by thirsty plants or trees, by the coconut (because it has eyes), and by ghosts and spirits who envy the living. It can shatter stones, poison or spoil food, and make fruit trees wither and die.

Envy or covetousness of livestock may cause blood to appear in a cow's milk or cause a pregnant mare to miscarry.

Misers are, by tradition, carriers of the evil eye. In India, if one meets a miser he goes without food the whole day to counteract the meeting.

Childless people are thought to envy those who have offspring, and desire for a child can cause a woman to covet the children of others. In India, even a childless old couple, long past their fertile years, is suspect.

"THOU SHALT NOT COVET"

The Ten Commandments appear twice in the Hebrew Bible: at Exodus 20:2–17 and Deuteronomy 5:6–21. According to the story in Exodus, they were revealed to Moses at Mount Sinai; modern scholars note that they may be modelled on earlier Hittite or Mesopotamian lists. In any case, they are Middle Eastern and they contain several warnings against envy. *"Thou shalt not covet thy neighbour's house; thou shalt not covet thy neighbour's wife, or his slaves, or his animals, or anything of thy neighbour."* To those who encounter Christianity outside the context of Jewish evil eye belief, God's reproach to covetousness seems a bit prim and fussy, but as other passages in the Bible show, the injunction is actually meant to prevent the evil eye.

"ENVENOMED EXHALATIONS" IN ANCIENT GREECE

In the 4th century Greek novel *"Æthiopica,"* the author, Heliodorus of Emesa, wrote: *"When any one looks at what is excellent with an envious eye he fills the surrounding atmosphere with a pernicious quality, and transmits his own envenomed exhalations into whatever is nearest to him."*

THE ENVIOUS EYE AND DEATH IN AFRICA

The influence of the evil eye is so keenly felt and is so much a part of the life of many African cultures that it affects every activity.

If a man be an unusually good hunter, he knows that if he returns to the village each day with a full bag of food he will arouse the envy of someone who has been less fortunate, leaving himself open to an attack of the evil eye. Because of this, he will not, even when he can do so, bring home more food than he can use in one day. By refraining from a display, he will not arouse envy and thus will be spared any designs which someone might hold against him. If he does fall prey to the evil eye despite his precautions, he is thought to have been bewitched through the malice of some person, even though that person may be unconscious of the fact. Quite often the one accused of sending the evil eye is innocent of anything but envy.

In *"Journal Des Missions Evangeliques"* Mme. Beguin tells the factual story of the death of the twelve-year-old son of a Barotse king, in Zambia. It was essential that the people find the cause of the boy's death, so they asked all who might throw light upon the subject. Quite by chance it was learned that a few days before the boy fell ill, a man had asked him for some milk and the boy had refused. "What will you do with the milk?" the man asked. That was enough; an evil spell had been cast upon the boy by the utterance of these words. An adult would never have refused the man a drink of milk, for he would have feared exposure to just such an envious glance as was thought to have been cast upon the boy by the thirsty man.

THE ENVIOUS EYE AND BLINDNESS IN AMERICA

Among the Pueblo Indians it is said that envy is a common motive for witchcraft. There was, early in the 20th century, a certain Sun shaman or medicine man among the Pueblo people called Gawire of Laguna who was blind. It was believed and often related that his blindness had been caused by less successful medicine men who were envious of his prestige. In this case, their evil eyes literally blinded him.

THE EYE OF UNUSUAL APPEARANCE

Certain types of eyes are thought to be more likely to inflict the evil eye than others, and thus accusations of casting the evil eye can be made against the rich and the poor, the high and the low, the good and the bad.

- **One Eye:** A person with only one eye is considered especially malignant when it comes to casting the evil eye.
- **Cross-Eyes and Wall-Eyes:** Those who have cross-eye (esotropic strabismus) or wall-eye (exotropic strabismus) are thought to have the evil eye, even if they mean no harm, because they "look askance" when their eyes are at rest.
- **Lazy Eyes and Squint Eyes:** Lazy eye (ambliopia) is a visual defect that leads to reduced vision in one eye. Those who have it cannot focus on an object with both eyes, so they may keep the weak or "lazy" eye shut, resulting in "squint eye," a generic term for the evil eye.
- **Double Pupils:** Polycoria or pupula duplex is an abnormality in which the eye has two pupils; Pliny the Elder identified it with the evil eye.
- **Bloodshot Eyes:** People who have little red veins showing in the white of the eyeballs are said to be able to inflict the evil eye, and this belief in the red "snake-eye" dates back to ancient Sumer.
- **Deep-Set Eyes:** Those whose eyes are set deep in theirs skulls, under bushy brows, are thought to be capable of casting the evil eye, inflicting a "penetrating gaze," "withering glance," or "death stare."
- **Heavy Eyebrows:** Eyes under a pair of eyebrows that meet in the center are feared. They seem angry, and the person is thought to be "looking daggers" or giving a "dirty look."
- **Blue Eyes:** Because blue eyes are rare in certain populations they are considered dangerous. Brown-eyed people tend to view blue-eyed people as bearers of the evil eye, probably because blue-eyed strangers who don't understand regional customs may praise and coo over babies, putting them at risk from the evil eye. Such strangers are also accused, behind their backs, of wanting to steal children.
- **Women's Eyes:** Among the Hindus, women's eyes are said to be more dangerous than men's although a woman's eyes do not usually become dangerous until she marries. The washerwoman, the oil seller, and the wife of the goldsmith are considered particularly dangerous.

THE PROJECTIVE EVIL EYE

Despite all the known rituals to prevent or remove the evil eye, there are people who will still continue to radiate evil eye influences.

THE PROJECTIVE EYE IN AFRICA

Among the Azande of the Belgian Congo, a wizard is one who possesses the evil eye and who, by a power inherent in him, exerts a bad influence, occasions misfortunes, and brings about illness and death. It is believed that people possessing this power may not be aware of it but that one who is aware of it can recognize the power in others.

Many Africans, including the Azande, the Fang or Pahuims, and the people of Ethiopia, Gabon, Ngoma or Namibia, Botswana, and Rwanda, believe that a wizard can project the eye to wreak havoc at a distance. They believe that within him lies a certain occult power which enables the eye of the wizard to leave the body and travel a considerable distance to work its influence upon any chosen subject. This occult power is attributed to some function of the body, some special organ or some bodily mechanism with which the wizard is thought to be endowed by nature.

Because of this belief, it is customary among the people mentioned above to perform an autopsy upon the bodies of wizards who die, in an endeavour to find the special mechanism which gave them their power when alive. Autopsy is common among Africans, not so much to study the organs to determine from what illness the late brother died, but to ascertain what wizard "ate the soul" of the departed. Thus, those who survive an attack may be warned against that wizard, who might have had similar designs against them.

THE PROJECTIVE EYE AMONG AFRICAN-AMERICANS

Among African-Americans, the African belief in the projective power of the covetous or jealous eye has been retained. It goes under a variety of regional names, including the Squint Eye, the Stink Eye, the Side Eye, the Long Eye, and the Whammy. If the Whammy is projected from both eyes, it is called the Double Whammy.

During the 20th century, a special hoodoo oil, sold to protect against the effects of the evil eye, was marketed under the name "Squint Drops." The label showed a White man in a cowboy hat squinting one eye.

THE PROJECTIVE EYE AMONG SICILIANS

In Sicily, especially among people of partial African, Moorish, or Jewish descent, it is believed that some people have the ability to project the evil eye. While elsewhere in Italy the evil eye is called *malocchio* or "bad eye," in Sicily it is *"jettatura,"* and one who projects it is a *"jettatore."* These terms come from the Indo-European root-word *ye* ("to throw or impel"), which is found in the English words eject, ejaculate, projection, and trajectory. In other words, *jettatore* are "projectors" and their specific form of evil eye is *jettatura* or "projection," in contradistinction to the Italian *malocchio* ("bad eye").

THE PROJECTIVE EYE OF THE INNOCENT

Jettatores are not necessarily evil or envious people, according to the Sicilian belief system, and they are often represented as being saddened and embarrassed by the harm they cause. At least two former Catholic pontiffs — Pope Pius IX and his successor Pope Leo XIII — were said to have projected the evil eye involuntarily, and Pius in particular was thought to have caused many deaths by his gaze.

In India as well it is not considered out of place to accuse a saintly man of having an evil eye. There are often instances of an ascetic who does penance for many days who, before he completes his penance, must take precautions against hurting anyone by his evil eye. Usually a pot of water is placed before him and he must gaze upon it so that the evil will go into the pot. Ashes are also used to absorb the evil.

Among the Hindus even divine images may inflict evil eye. In the Banashankari Devi Temple in the state of Karnataka there is an image of the goddess Banashankari, the sixth incarnation of the warrior-goddess Durga, which is avoided by pregnant women. Certain images of Shiva as well are worshipped blindfolded as a protection against his evil eye.

Pride also leads to the innocent evil eye. In India, when the first child arrives the father cannot look upon it before a piece of gold is placed upon the child to protect it from the parental pride in the father's eye.

Even love itself is not omitted from the list. In many traditional Indian marriage ceremonies the bride and bridegroom are shielded one from the other by a curtain or a veil, lest in their love they injure one another.

Finally, there is such a thing as inflicting evil eye upon oneself! This can be done by gazing in admiration at oneself in a mirror too frequently.

Cover art for "Unmasking Fear" by Charles M. Quinlan, a 1949 reprint from Lormar Press of a small part of the Spiritualist book *"God's World"* by Lloyd Kenyon Jones, first pubished in 1919.

THE EVIL EYE'S EFFECTS ON CHILDREN

THE JEWISH MOTHER GUARDS HER CHILD
If a Jewish child is taken outside or is seen by non-family members before the age of 40 days and falls sick, the evil eye may be strongly suspected. If someone praised the child and the mother did not immediately refuse the compliment, kiss the child with wet lips or spit on him, or say "peh-peh-peh" while pretending to spit, or say *"kein ayin hara"* ("no evil eye" in Yiddish), then the mother erred.

THE EFFECT OF THE EVIL EYE ON CHILDREN IN INDIA
In India, children are claimed to possess *shakti* or special power to avert the evil eye and so one often sees the drawing of a child on the door of the home to protect it. In the same manner of reasoning, earth taken from the doorsteps of a person who is thought to cast the evil eye is brought to a child to look upon, which we call "the showing cure," and which is unique to India. It is then burned in a fire. Yet, mark this inconsistency in Indian folklore! Above we have two examples wherein the child is thought to possess powers to neutralize and overcome the evil eye, yet despite this, the child is given every possible protection AGAINST the influence by means of amulets and charms.

THE EVIL EYE'S EFFECTS ON MOTHERS

THE MOTHER AS THE PROTECTORESS
Because the mother is a source of liquids — birth fluids, breast milk, menstrual blood, saliva, and tears — it is the mother, or a mother-goddess, in whom trust is placed to protect the vulnerable ones in a family. It is she who burns the Aspand, spits on the child, knows the rituals, rolls the egg over the victim, or seeks out an elder woman to help her with the cure.

THE MOTHER AS THE VICTIM
If a pregnant woman is envied, she may have a miscarriage, If a mother dresses her child too well or boasts too much, she invites envy upon the child and also upon herself. Her breast milk may dry up, she may become infertile, and she may become a dessicated old woman well before her time.

THE EVIL EYE'S EFFECTS ON WOMEN

A WITHERING GLANCE
Aside from their time of motherhood, vain women place themselves on display and invite jealous glances at their bosoms, hair, or faces. Covering these portions of the female figure to avert envy is an old tradition, and is not solely the result of male possessiveness over subjugated wives.

THE EVIL EYE'S EFFECTS ON MEN

PROTECTING THE PENIS
The portion of a man most subject to envy is the penis, and the result is impotence and infertility. Male gestures like the corno or fig protect the penis, as do amulets that represent such gestures. The hamsa, eye-in-hand, and girdle of Isis offer revivifying sanctuary in the moist female genitalia.

THE EVIL EYE'S EFFECTS ON ANIMALS

EQUINE SUSCEPTIBILITY TO THE EVIL EYE
Because they are seen by the public, horses, ponies, donkeys, and mules require protection from envy lest they succumb to colic. Blue donkey beads guard the donkeys of Iran, the Kalbeliyas of India hang mirror-charms on their horses, and the Jewish Talmud recommends a red thread braided into the horse's forelock and hung between its eyes.

AQUARIUM-DWELLERS ARE IMMUNE
Fish are not affected by the evil eye. Your aquarium pets are safe.

THE EVIL EYE'S EFFECTS ON PLANTS

SUSCEPTIBLE AND PROTECTIVE PLANTS
Some trees, plants, grains, and flowers avert the evil eye, but some must be protected. Fruit trees are susceptible to envy, and will drop unripe fruit if afflicted. Flowers wither if subjected to an envious gaze. Rue, Lemons, Ajvan Caraway, Cloves, and Fennel will avert the evil eye. Aspand and Cloves, if popped on charcoal, will destroy it and affect a cure.

THE EVIL EYE'S EFFECTS ON EATING

HINDU FOOD CUSTOMS TO AVOID THE EVIL EYE
- Some religious Brahmins eat in silence, and conversation only begins when the meal has ended. This reduces envious gazes at the meal.
- Many Hindus drink only when they have finished a meal, pouring the water into their mouths. Water covers the evil eye.
- Some Hindus do not save left-overs; rather these are thrown to passing animals, such as crows and dogs, to avert their evil eye.
- Food is seldom carried outdoors, or if it is, it is covered. While meals are prepared, the doors are closed. When carrying milk, a blade of grass or lump of charcoal in the pail is as effective as a covering.

JEWISH FOOD CUSTOMS TO AVOID THE EVIL EYE
- The Book of Proverbs 23:6 reads, *"Eat thou not the bread of him that hath an evil eye,"* so Jews tend to bring gifts of baked goods to a meal.
- When dining out, among Jews it is commonplace to either give money to beggars who stand around restaurants or to offer to buy them a meal, lest their jealousy create a complaint before the throne of God.
- To avoid envy over food, Jews offer others extra helpings or "a little taste" from their own plates, with courtesy phrases like, "Eat! Eat!"
- The hole in a bagel roll looks like an eye, so bagels protect their eaters.
- The braided challah Sabbath bread is kept covered before blessing it.

MUSLIM FOOD CUSTOMS TO AVOID THE EVIL EYE
- Setting two onions before the dishes protects food against the eye.
- To avoid envy, servants receive the same food as their employers.
- A bridal pair may be served food under a blanket to protect them.
- Left-over food is put in a pot with broom straws, grass from the roof of a house, earth from below the hinges of a door, and dust from a crossroads. This is set on fire, waved three time around the eaters, three times toward the Sun, and then turned upside-down.

AMERICAN FOOD CUSTOMS TO AVOID THE EVIL EYE
- Pet dogs may give the evil eye by hungrily watching people prepare food, so cooks throw them fried dough-balls before the meal is served. These ameliorative offerings are called "hush-puppies" in the South.

WHEN THE EVIL EYE IS POWERLESS

ASHKENAZI JEWS: LOAVES AND FISHES

Jews whose surname includes the word "fish," in any language are immune to the evil eye because fishes, who live under water, are not affected by the evil eye, and it is powerless against them. Those born under the zodiacal Sun sign of Pisces, the Fishes, also do not get the evil eye.

All of the descendants of Joseph, son of Jacob, are immune to the evil eye. Naming a child Josef or Joseph conveys protection from the eye.

Envy is at the root of the Jewish custom (codified in religious law) of not allowing a father and his son, two brothers, or two half-brothers of the same mother to be successively called up to read the Torah before the congregation, because "an orphan or a father who has lost his son may be reminded of his loss, feel jealousy, and give *ayin hara*."

One exception to this custom is made during the Feast of Purim, when the Scroll of Esther (*"Megillat Esther"*) is read in its lengthy entirety (the whole megillah!) — and not once, but twice, which is such a superfluity of Torah reading that everyone gets a turn and no jealousy will be engendered. Furthermore, if a child takes sick during the feast of Purim, the evil eye is ruled out as a cause because no one gets *ayin hara* during Purim.

Another way to disempower the eye is to cover food, especially the two loaves of braided bread called challah, served at the Sabbath meal. These are covered with a special cloth before the meal. There are two reasons:

According to Rabbi Yisrœl Salanter Lipkin (1809-1883), a baker told him, "When there are many different foods on the table, the first blessing is always made over the bread, after which no other blessing need be made. On Friday night, however, the first blessing has to be made over the wine. In order not to shame the challah, who expects the blessing to be made over her, we must cover her over until after the sanctification of the wine." Here the cover stops the challah from looking with envy upon the wine.

The second reason for covering the bread is that a pair of braided challah is something women take pride in, and if another woman sees such loaves she may envy them, and hungry people may covet them as well. Covering the challah preserves it from envy until it is cut, which mars its perfection.

Alas, the challah cloth itself may become a source of pride and envy, for some women are expert embroiderers and ornately ornament their challah covers. But "better that the cloth takes a hit than the bread."

JOSEPH SON OF JACOB: THE COVERING OF WATER

Joseph was a prophetic dreamer and hydromancer. His magic was so powerful that when he died the Egyptians placed his bones in a metal casket and sank it like a giant amulet in a secret place in the Nile river to both bless the river and keep the Hebrews enslaved. Generations later it was located by Serach bat Asher, and with his bones, the Jews escaped from Egypt.

Neither Joseph himself nor his descendants are subject to the evil eye. There are two reasons.

The first reason is rooted in Genesis 49:22, *"Joseph is a fruitful vine, a fruitful vine by a fountain; its branches run over the wall."* However, because of the poetic vagaries of the Hebrew language, early rabbinical sages gave this interpretation: *"Joseph is a fruitful vine that rises above the eye; its branches run over the wall."* Note the play on words between the watery fountain and the eye.

The second reason given by rabbinical sages comes from Genesis 48:16. In blessing Joseph's sons, Jacob says, *"And let them grow like fish into a multitude in the midst of the earth."* So just as fish in the sea are covered by water and the evil eye has no power over them, Joseph's descendants are also covered. These same sages also ruled that it is effective to simply say or write the claim, *"I come from the descendants of Joseph, over whom the evil eye has no dominion."* Some amulets are merely marked with the name "Joseph" in any linguistic equivalent, and that is enough.

SERACH BAT ASHER: INTERCESSOR AGAINST THE EYE

To the Mizrahi Jews of Persian descent, Serach bat Asher is an evil eye fighting hero. Often depicted playing her harp, she is one of the few people believed to have ascended to heaven without dying. She was given the gift of immortality during a blessing by Jacob when she told him the good news that his favourite son, Joseph, remained alive.

Serach's ability to see beneath the water to locate Joseph's lost casket demonstrates that her power is even greater than that of the evil eye. For this reason, her name is often invoked on amulets. She is still highly venerated in Isfahan — the city from which she left Earth in 1133 CE — and it is believed that she continues to make earthly visits.

Because of her immortality, many consider Serach bat Asher to be the embodiment of collective Jewish memory and knowledge, and an extremely helpful intercessor in the battle against the evil eye.

AMERICA: "DON'T JINX IT"
In the United States we often hear that one should not announce a plan, a pregnancy, or a new job, lest we "jinx it."

INDIA: SECRECY ENDS THE POWER OF THE EYE
In India, exposure is the surest way to become affected by the evil eye, so Hindus take pains not to expose themselves, their families, their food, or their worldly possessions to the glances of those who may covet them. Because secrecy undermines the evil eye, the object of a journey is kept a secret, items that bring undue admiration are given away, and a father is not allowed to see his newborn child for from five to twelve days after birth.

SAUDI ARABIA: SECRET WEDDING PLANS
Muslim women in Saudi Arabia who want their daughters to prosper hold the great hope that they will go to university, get a good job, and marry well. If this does not happen as wished and planned, it is obvious that the evil eye is on the young woman. Those who have seen this happen learn from the experience of family and friends to keep announcements of graduation and career advancement secret, but above all to not make announcements when a man asks for their daughter's hand in marriage. Nothing should be announced until plans are finalized.

THE MAORI: A SECRET JOURNEY
Among the Maori of New Zealand, when a person falls sick and is thought to have been laid low by the evil eye, "a change of air" is prescribed. It is thought that if the person goes to a region where he is unknown he can lose the demons on the way. In such cases the idea is to remove the patient entirely from the locality where the evil influence has arisen and from the influence of anyone who caused the affliction. Such a journey is usually made in secrecy, the destination is secret, and the patient is unaccompanied by even a close relative or friend.

AMERICA: FEARLESS LAUGHTER
Americans who say they do not believe in the evil eye actually acknowledge its existence when they boast that the eye is powerless to harm a person who does not fear it. Laughter, they claim, will destroy the eye. Not all Americans believe this, of course.

3. PRECAUTIONS

In the previous pages we have dealt with the manner in which the evil eye operates. We have observed that in addition to a direct glance, a sideglance, or an overlong envious gaze, the evil eye may be interpreted more broadly as a hidden thought in the mind and as a projected energetic force. We have also noted the conditions under which the evil eye is most powerful, and when it is thought to be powerless.

Now, if one person believes that another person wishes him harm and if harm does befall them, he concludes that his belief must be correct. But by then it may be too late; the evil will have been done.

It can be easily seen that it is difficult to control the envious thoughts of others. You cannot tell people NOT to harbour jealousy or NOT to think evil of you. That just will not work. But then again, perhaps your suspicions were unfounded and the evil was a mere coincidence. You cannot go around making accusations against innocent people and blaming them for every little accident or bad stroke of luck that comes along.

Because of this peculiarity of psychology, a complex system of arts and rituals has been built up by working on the principle that if one cannot control another's thoughts, then a method must be devised to render these thoughts harmless or neutralized BEFORE an attack is made.

This psychological device is much the same as if you wore a bulletproof vest. Such a precautionary measure would not stop a person from shooting at you but it very well might render the bullet harmless.

AVOIDING EVIL ANIMALS

In Africa, it is not human beings alone who have the power to cast the evil eye. An animal may be the culprit. If a hornbill alights upon a house it is an omen of ill fortune and all within range of its vision must be purified. Chief among the African animals who are thought to project the eye are the manatee and the fox — and the latter is notable among Jews as well, for the Talmud recommends hanging the tail of a fox on a horse to repel envy.

In India a species of harmless snake called the daman or Indian rat snake, along with the owl, the cat, the dog, and the crow, may do evil with their eyes, and some Brahmins offer a portion of their sacrificial meals to the crows to avert their evil eyes.

DON'T LET THE BABY BE SEEN FOR 40 DAYS

Among Jews and Muslims it is said that for the first forty days of a baby's life it should not be seen in public, nor should guests be invited to the home. The folkloric explanation for this precaution is that "someone may envy the baby," but a secondary reason may be given by way of Biblical analogy: "Just as Noah floated on the waters for forty days and the children of Isræl wandered for forty years in the wilderness, so is the baby not yet fully in the physical world until forty days have passed."

Some families add extra precautions: The mother does not hold the child on her lap or nurse it when guests are present. Instead, the child lays upon a pillow in her lap, and on the pillowcase, or embroidered into it, a red thread must be visible, to distract the evil eye. In India, a similar custom calls for laying the baby on the now-infertile mother-in-law's old sari cloth.

GUARDING THE GARDEN FROM ENVIOUS EYES

In India, in past times, a gardener would refuse admittance to his garden until the guests washed their eyes to remove all possibility of the evil eye, because an envious glance might cause his blossoms to wither or his crops to fail. Presenting the visitor with flowers or garden crops, while ostensibly just a friendly gesture, is also a way to assuage the eyes of the covetous.

THE WARNING IN A COCONUT

In India, a Hindu about to take a journey, who accidentally looks upon a coconut, might immediately call the whole thing off because the "eyes" of the coconut would portend an ominous outcome.

SOMETHING BORROWED, SOMETHING BLUE

The Anglo-American rhyme that tells brides to wear *"something old, something new, something borrowed, something blue"* is in part a precaution against the evil eye. "Something old" mitigates the bride's enviable finery, "something new" marks her embarkation on married life, "something borrowed" is the undergarment of a woman who has already had a baby, to misdirect any envy of her fertility, and "something blue" is the protective colour of water, against which the evil eye cannot prevail. In England a third line may added to the couplet: *"and a sixpence in her shoe."* The shoe is protective against the evil eye — see page 56 for shoes on wedding vehicles — and the sixpence is a lucky coin in England.

PROHIBITIONS AGAINST LOOKING

The gift of sight among the people of India may be more appreciated than it is among most other peoples. Americans, for instance, take it for granted. Its full significance is not often appreciated until it is lost or at least until it begins to fail. With most Americans, seeing is merely an essential to living a full life or accomplishing one's daily work.

To many in India the gift of sight has far greater significance. Sight transmits qualities. More than that, the sense of sight can be both active and passive, good and bad. In other words, it can be as dangerous to look at a person or thing as it is dangerous to be looked upon by another.

It can be seen, then, that sight has a quality or character just as an individual has certain qualities of good or evil. This quality is *shakti* and it may be defined as "active, inherent power or energy." When this *shakti* is good it conveys goodness, good luck, good fortune, and blessings. When this *shakti* is bad it can generate *drishti,* the evil eye.

Many Indians undertake regular rituals of purification. After performing these rites it is considered evil to look back at the spot once the ritual is completed. To do so would be to bring bad luck or some misfortune. In the same manner, while bringing herbs or sanctified water to a spot to effect a cure or charm, it is forbidden to look backwards. Pall-bearers bearing a corpse must not look back at the house from which it has been taken, and when returning from a funeral it is also forbidden to look back at the site of the funeral as this might bring misfortune. African-American root doctors also caution against looking back at the site where one has cast a spell.

Other prohibitions along similar lines include cautioning a pregnant woman against looking upon certain things and forbidding unclean persons to gaze at any heavenly bodies.

PRECAUTIONS AGAINST EVIL SPIRITS

In India, not only people and animals, but also ghosts and spirits, may give the evil eye, and when people say that someone is "possessed by spirits," they may mean he was given the eye. Many a Hindu mother will wave a little salt around her child, saying, "May the evil eye of strangers, ghosts, spirits, and also of parents and relatives be averted." It can be seen from the chant of the mother that ghosts, spirits, and even the parents of the child are included as possible sources. Thus the evil eye is a common threat which it all humans must accept and do their best to avoid at all times.

4. AVERTING THE EYE

AVERTING THE EYE WITH WORDS

THE PRIESTLY BLESSING
The text of the priestly blessing in the Book of Numbers 6:24–26 is considered effective against the evil eye: *"The Lord bless thee, and keep thee. The Lord make his face shine upon thee, and be gracious unto thee. The Lord lift up his countenance upon thee, and give thee peace."*

THE LETTER N AND FISHES IN THE PSALMS
In Hebrew, the letter "N" is pronounced "nun." In Aramaic, the word *"nun"* means "fish." Since "fish are immune to the evil eye because they live under water," Jews recite Bible verses which both start and end with the letter *nun* to ward off the evil eye. Among these are Psalms 46:5, Psalms 77:5, and Psalms 78:2 — but they are only effective if recited in Hebrew.

AVERSIVE PHRASES
When a Jew wishes to praise a person, animal, or object without any taint of envy, he may begin with the Hebrew phrase, *"bli ayin hara"* ("without the the evil eye"). However, if a person, child, animal, or object is praised without that ameliorating phrase, then to annul any possible envy, he may say, *"kein ayin hara"* ("no evil eye" in Yiddish).

THE SEED OF JOSEPH
If someone has cast the evil eye on you, you can close your hands over your crossed thumbs and silently say, *"I come from the seed of Joseph, over whom the evil eye has no power, as it is written, Joseph is a fruitful vine, a fruitful vine above the eye."*

JACOB'S BLESSING ON THE SONS OF JOSEPH
Jacob's blessing on the sons of Joseph in Genesis 48:16 is spoken over boys: *"The Angel which redeemed me from all evil, bless the lads ... and let them grow into a multitude in the midst of the earth."* The literal translation of "grow into a multitude" is "multiply like fishes," and so as fishes are immune to the evil eye, the boys will be as well.

AVERTING THE EYE WITH GESTURES

Gestures that are used to avert the evil eye come in four basic types:

- Gestures that threaten to pierce or harm the eye
- Gestures that protectively conceal the phallic thumb
- Gestures that mislead the eye into thinking the envied item is unclean.
- Gestures that surreptitiously or openly moisten the envied item.

THE GESTURE OF STRETCHING OUT THE HAND
A custom which we find in India and around the whole wide world is that of stretching out the hand in the face of one who is thought to possess the power of the evil eye. This action is much the same as the palms-down position in which the hypnotist stretches out his hands before the face of a subject.

In India, this gesture is called *bujo* or *bhundo*. In Karnataka, the women use the gesture of the outstretched hand and say, *"Let fingers be thrust in your eye."* In the Deccan, on the other hand, the gesture is accompanied by, "May there be a sore in your eye."

We find this same gesture used in Algeria, Tunisia, Syria, Israel, Palestine, Greece, Italy, and among the Sennaarese and Kababish people of Sudan. In nearly every instance, but particularly in Algeria, Tunisia, and Syria, the gesture is accompanied by the words: "Five in your eye," "Five on your eye," "Five on you," or "Five in the face of the enemies." In Arabic, the word "five" is *hamsa*, and thus the spoken phrase may refer to the hamsa hand, a protective amulet.

This custom can be traced back many generations. The ancient Romans used the same gesture, along with the phrase: *"Ecce tibi dono quinque."* ("See, I give you five.")

The modern custom of "thumbing the nose" at an enemy undoubtedly had its origin in this ancient custom as well, for the same general sentiment is involved in each case.

THE PALM UP GESTURE
In Greece, when one suspects the evil eye, the right hand is held palm upward with the fingers spread and then thrust sharply forward. Some people also say, *"Skata sta moutra sou!"* ("Shit in your face!")

THE MANO FICA OR FIG HAND GESTURE

The fig hand gesture or Mano Fica (sometimes improperly rendered as Mano Fico) consists of inserting the phallic thumb between the first and middle fingers and closing them around it, so that only the tip protrudes. The symbol is one of penis-in-vagina intercourse, but the meaning is the protection of the penis from desiccation by enveloping it in the womb-like fig-hand. This gesture is also embodied in the form of a protective amulet.

THE DOUBLE FIG GESTURE

According to the Jewish rabbis who wrote the Talmud, the double fig gesture is recommended as a remedy against the evil eye. In Talmud Berakhot 55b it is written, *"Whoever is afraid to enter a city because of the evil eye should clasp the right thumb in the fingers of the left hand and the thumb of the left hand in the fingers of the right hand while saying, 'I, so-and-so, son of so-and-so, am of the seed of Joseph, over whom the evil eye has no dominion.'"* To make this gesture, hold the hands upright with palms outward and thumbs crossing one another, then close the fingers of each hand on the opposite hand's thumb. The result is a "double fig," or the protection of both phallic thumbs within both female fig-hands.

THE CORNO OR HORN GESTURE

In Italy, it is believed that one can avert the evil eye of a *jettatore* by pointing two fingers at them. This is done by extending the index finger and little finger, then curling the middle and ring fingers toward the palm and holding them down with the thumb. The result looks like the horned head of an animal. Because Pope Pius IX was thought to be a *jettatore*, those who received a blessing from him often secretly made the corno or horn gesture to ward off the evil eye. The gesture is also embodied in the form of a protective amulet.

THE GESTURE OF RENDERING THE CHILD DIRTY

In India, when going out of doors, a mother will take earth from beneath the feet of her child and rub it on his face, for a dirty child is less likely to be envied. In Scotland, a mother guards against *droch shuil* by making her child wear torn clothing, or at least one sock inside-out.

THE GESTURE OF PUTTING SALIVA ON A "DIRTY" CHILD

Ashkenazi Jewish mothers counteract the "dryness" of the evil eye while also rendering their children dirty, and thus less prone to jealousy. If someone praises the baby, the mother licks her first finger, or first and middle fingers, or kisses them to cover the act of licking, and pretends to rub dirt from the child's face. To the one who complimented the child she may say, half in English and half in Yiddish, "Oh, she would look pretty, if she were not so *smutzig* (dirty)." By this act the child is rendered too dirty to covet and also receives life-giving moisture from the mother.

THE GESTURE OF SPITTING ON THE GROUND

Jews often react to a compliment that might carry the tinge of envy, especially if it is given to a child, by spitting on the ground three times. In this manner, wetness is applied in the general direction of the child, without touching it or holding the one who praised it responsible.

THE MIMICRY OF SPITTING AS A GESTURE

In contemporary society, spitting on the ground is seen as unsanitary, and in any case spitting might inform the one who made a compliment that the evil eye was suspected, and so the wise Jewish parent engages in the mimicry of spitting, without actually releasing saliva from the mouth. Regional sound-effects are used in this gesture of imitation spitting. Some say "Feh! Feh! Feh!" or "Pu! Pu! Pu!," some say "Tu! Tu! Tu!," and some make a wet "Theh! Theh! Theh!" sound. Turning away from the one who voiced the compliment and making the gesture over the left shoulder will further defuse the implication that *ayin hara* was intended. The person who made the *faux pas* may then say *"bli ayin hara"* ("without the evil eye") or *"kein ayin hara"* ("no evil eye").

THE SPIT AND WAVE GESTURE

In India people spit three times on their fingertips and each time make a quick waving and shaking movement with the hands to repel the eye.

THE GESTURE OF SPRINKLING WATER

To avoid the evil eye, Moroccan Muslims sprinkle water on the seats where envious people sat while visting and also sprinkle the door with water after envious people have left their home.

AVERTING THE EYE WITH RITUALS

THE ZOROASTRIAN RITUAL OF ESPHAND OR ASPAND

Throughout the former Persian Empire, including modern Iran, Iraq, and Central Asia, a seed called Aspand, Espand, Esphand, Urzerlik, or Syrian Rue *(Peganum harmala)* is used to rid people, especially children, of the evil eye, and to bring blessings after a sorrowful task, such as attending a funeral. This ancient ritual is of Zoroastrian origin, but is popular with Muslims. It is performed by dropping Aspand and, alone or mingled with Frankincense and herbs, on hot charcoal, where it pops and gives off a great deal of fragrant smoke. A five-line rhyming spell calls on King Naqshband, a Muslim replacement for the earlier Zoroastrian archangel Spenta Armaiti, embodying Espand. The smoke is swirled around the recipient's heads seven times to protect him and remove the evil eye.

Aspand balla band
Ba haq shah-e-Naqshband
Chashm-e-aaish chashm-e-khaysh
Chashm-e-adam-e bad andaysh
Besuzad dar atash-e-taiz

This is Aspand, it banishes the evil eye
By the blessing of King Naqshband
Eyes of nothing, eyes of relatives
Eyes of friends, eyes of enemies
Should burn in this glowing fire.

AVERTING THE EYE WITH AMULETS

A mother whose child has once been struck by the evil eye will soon take the advice of the other women in her community and acquire an amulet for the child to wear to repel the evil eye in the future. This sort of charm is called an apotropaic talisman. Their designs vary from one area to another. The simplest are threads or cords; more conspicuous are the amulets, often in the form of an eye, hand, horseshoe, or a combination of elements, such as the eye-in-hand and horseshoe-and-eyes, and regionally popular charms, such as the hamsa hand and martenitsa.

AMULETS: THE COLOUR RED

Amulets of red symbolize the menstrual blood or birth fluids of a goddess like Isis, a folk-deity like Baba Marta, or a revered matriarch such as Rachel. The girdle or buckle of Isis, martenisa, and bendel string are red.

WRIST BAND FROM THE TOMB OF RACHEL
In 20th century Isræl, narrow strips of white cloth, block-printed in red Hebrew letters, "[From] the Tomb of Rachel," were wound around the tomb to bless them, then cut into segments and sold as anti-evil-eye souvenirs.

THE JEWISH BENDEL OR "KABBALAH STRING"
The *bendel* ("band"), *tzamid kabbalah* ("kabbalah bracelet") or *chut hashemi* ("string of the name [of God]") is a wristlet of red wool or cotton string. You can make your own or purchase one made from string that was wrapped around Rachel's Tomb seven times before being cut.

AMULETS: THE COLOUR BLUE

Amulets of blue represent water, which covers and protects fishes from the evil gaze, and reflects back the envy of a blue-eyed person. Hamsa hand, eye-in-hand, wadjet eye, and scarab beetle charms are often blue.

BLUE BEADS
From India through Europe, blue beads are a potent talisman when worn as armlets or necklaces. In Bulgaria, for instance, plain blue beads, beads with eyes (ujikos), a hamsa, and a religious book are put under the pillow of the baby to protect it. The Turks have their blue glass nazar boncugu and Iranians prize their blue faience donkey beads.

BLUE PAINT, BLUE BOTTLES, AND LAUNDRY BLUEING
African-Americans may paint porch ceilings "haint blue" to keep off evil or make bottle trees from blue Milk of Magnesia bottles. Blue glass witch bottles filled with nails and broken glass sit on the window sill. Laundry blueing is added to wash water and baths and can be used to dress the soles of the feet. In Trinidad, a packet of blueing is pinned to the baby's clothes.

Buckle of Isis

Evil Eye Charm

Eye Agate

Eye in Hand

Fascinus

Hamsa Hand

Mano Cornuto

Mano Figa

Wedjat or Utchat Eye

THREAD, STRING, AND CORD CHARMS

RED CORDS AND THREADS
Female blood or anything red has the power to avert the evil eye, so red cords worn around the neck or wrist protect babies in the Middle East, Europe, and India. The Romani of Romania and Bulgaria wear a red cord bracelet, with or without a blue eye-bead on it, much like the Jewish bendel.

TRI-COLOUR SILK ANKLETS WITH FIVE KNOTS
In India anklets made of red, green, and yellow silk which has been tied into five knots are a charm given to children to wear.

PURPLE OR RED THREAD OR EMBROIDERY
The Romans under the Emperor Albinus (about 196 A.D.) had a custom of wrapping newborn children in bandages of a reddish hue, and children up to the age of puberty were dressed in a special purple-bordered garment which had the power to avert the evil eye.

BLACK THREAD CHARMS AGANST DRISHTI
A potent talisman in India is a thread which has been hand spun from the wool of a black sheep. This may be tied around the wrist of a child to prevent the evil eye. Black cloth also protects. The chiild's umbilical cord may dried and cast into a metal pendant which is worn on a black string. Babies also have their eyes adorned with black kohl eyeliner.

WHEN THE STRING BREAKS
In India, blue bead charms are placed on newborn babies; when the string or cord breaks and the bead is lost, the child is old enough to have escaped the dangers of the evil eye. Jews say that when the string or chain holding a apotropaic charm breaks, "it took the hit for you." If not damaged, the amulet is given a new string or chain and can be worn again.

COWRIE SHELLS ON LEATHER CORDS
In Senegal people believe that beautiful objects break if they arouse envy, so they wear leather bracelets on which cowrie shells are sewn. The shells absorb evil and the leather darkens with negativity. When the cord breaks, it has saved something that otherwise would have been destroyed.

HOW TO MAKE A RED STRING BENDEL

A red thread bracelet or bendel with a blue bead on it is one of the most effective evil eye charms you can make. Traditional fibers are wool or cotton. You can spin your own yarn, but for a simple and easy method, try using pre-dyed crochet-weight red pearl cotton or red wool yarn. You can find these at any craft store, in person or online. Eighteen inches should be enough for most wrist sizes. You do not have to wind the yarn around the tomb of Rachel, but praying over it in Rachel's name is a good idea.

To ply the string, making a four-ply from a two-ply commercial yarn or pearl cotton, cut a length a little more than twice as long as needed. String your blue eye bead on it and position the bead at about the 1/4 mark. Now you are ready to overspin the yarn or pearl cotton.

Hold one end firmly and twirl the other end in the same direction it was originally spun to overspin it. It will get tighter and tighter. Keep it taut. When you can't overspin it any more, it will kink near the middle. Let it twirl around itself. Grasp the ends tightly, without releasing either end. Slide the blue bead to the position desired. Still holding the ends together tightly, stroke it smooth as it neatly plies itself. You can continue to twirl the ends if you wish a tighter ply. If it was two ply, it will now be four-ply.

Tie the ends together with an overhand knot and trim it. Then wrap the bracelet around your wrist and tie it on with square knots — either three or seven, according to your favoured family or regional tradition.

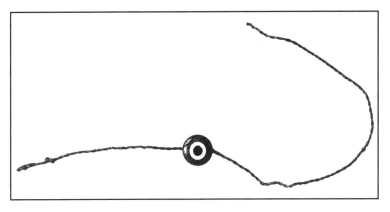

A twisted red string bendel with a turquoise-blue glass eye bead.

EYE AMULETS

THE ALL-SEEING EYE
A single human eye surrounded by radiating beams of light, called the All-Seeing Eye, found in many eras and cultures, is a symbol of the watchful and protective power of the Supreme Being. It appears on the Great Seal of the United States on the dollar bill, and is among the many beautiful symbols of Freemasonry, where it represents the Great Architect of the Universe. In its specifically protective role, the All-Seeing Eye appears on a well-known North American good luck token of the 1930s which is inscribed, "The All Seeing Eye Guards You From Evil."

EYE-AGATE OR LUK MIK STONES
The eye-agate, called the *luk mik* ("goat's eye") in Tibet, is a form of brown and white banded agate. If cut at the proper angle and shaped into a cabochon or lenticular bead, it can very closely resemble an eye. Eye-agates may be worn alone or incorporated into other jewellry charms.

EYE OF BUDDHA
In Nepal, where Vajrayana Buddhism mingles elements of Himalayan animist beliefs with reverence for Gautama Buddha, an amulet called the Eye of Buddha is worn to reflect back the eye. The center is an eye-agate.

DZI BEADS
Dzi beads, highly valued as charms in Tibet, originated in prehistoric times, perhaps in India or Persia. Carved of agate, they are decorated with designs of eyes and zig-zag lines, using an ancient process of heat and chemical treatment. Modern replica dzi beads have been crafted in China.

THE WADJET OR UDJAT EYE
Among the ancient Egyptians the eye of the god Horus, called the wadjet or udjat eye, was worn for protection. Although found in many materials, the most numerous are those of blue-glazed faience or steatite.

THE EERIE EYE
In American novelty catalogues one can often find the so-called "eerie eye charm" which is a life-like blue eye set in an eyelid-shaped bezel.

CAT'S EYE SHELLS

The cat's eye shell, which is the operculum or foot-closure of a sea-snail called a Turban Shell or Turbo, is widely used in Europe and the Middle East against the evil eye, no doubt because it resemble an eye. One species is a dull reddish-brown, the other a shiny greenish colour. Both are used as charms. During the Victorian era, they were made into amuletic jewelry. Because the shells have a natural cabochon shape, they were easily set into silver or gold rings or brooches, often made by or for British sailors and given as gifts to family and lovers. In America, cat--s eye shells are commonly found in African-American mojo bags prepared for protection from evil, for uncrossing, and to break a jinx.

BLUE NAZAR BONCUGU

In Greece and Turkey, the most common form of apotropaic charm is the blue glass eye charm called the *nazar boncugu* or *nazar boncuk* ("eye bead"), which mirrors back the evil eye and thus "confounds" it. Turks make beautiful blue blown glass nazar charms, as well as in regionally-specific forms like the horseshoe-and-eyes and eyes-all-over styles. Modern Turkish women wear jewelry-quality sterling silver evil eye bracelets, made not only in the traditional shades of blue, but in ultra-hip fashion colours. Turkish street vendors can be found who will write "Your Name on a Grain of Rice" and encase it in a blue-glass tube with a tiny nazar-bead stopper.

BLUE DONKEY BEADS

In Iran, large turquoise-blue beads of rough faience, called donkey beads, protect livestock from the evil eye. These beads had quite a moment of popularity in the 1960s when an enterprising Iranian rug merchant imported thousands of them to the San Francisco Bay Area, where hippies bought them and used them as statement beads in colourful necklaces. Gradually they disappeared, but one day in the 2000s, catherine saw three strings of donkey beads atop some Persian rugs at a trade show, and asked the seller about them. Now well over 80 years old, he was the Iranian rug merchant who had commissioned a floor tile shop to produce them, and brought them to the USA. Thirty years after he had sold out all his stock, he had found three strings hanging on a hook in his warehouse. Cat bought them all, at ten times the price she'd paid as a hippie jewelry-maker.

HAND AMULETS

ROMAN HAND OF POWER TALISMAN
One of the oldest forms of hand-talisman is the Roman hand of power, a bronze votary of a hand covered with symbolic images that was kept on the home altar to protect and bless the entire family.

MANO PODEROSA TALISMAN
In countries where Catholicism is the dominant religion, a Christianized version of the Roman hand of power is given traits of the eye-in-hand and the resultant image is called "the Most Powerful Hand of God" or *mano poderosa*. In this apotropaic charm — usually carried on the person in the form of a holy card or, in Peru, as a protective package amulet, the symbolic images that cover the hand have been replaced by saints and a gaping crucifixion wound suggests an eye in the palm.

MANO FICO OR FIGA CHARM
In Italy, when a man's potency is threatened by the evil eye, he may choose to wear or carry a red coral, gold, or silver hand charm making the *mano fico* ("Fig hand") gesture to repel the evil. These amulets are worn as necklaces, watch fobs, and pocket pieces by men and boys. In Brazil the fig hand charm is carved of black jet and is called the *figa*, which is Portuguese for "Fig." The charm is the embodiment of the ritual gesture of the mano fico or figa.

MANO CORNUTO CHARM
Another regionally popular hand amulet is the mano cornuto ("horned hand"). It is primarily found in Italy and in America among descendants of Italian immigrants. Mano cornuto charms are often made of pewter, as intentional reproductions of 19th century silver amulets, probably from the area around Naples, where this particular type of amulet has been extremely popular and was at one time available carved of blood coral. To many modern viewers, especially those not from a Mediterranean background, this hand gesture is known for its appearance in popular culture as the "Hook 'Em Horns," "Dr. Strange mystic gesture," "Spider-Man web-shooting gesture," "rock'n'roll hands," or "Satan hands." The charm is actually an embodiment of the mano cornuto gesture.

EYE-IN-HAND AMULET

In India, Pakistan, Isræl, Turkey, and the Arab countries, small models of a hand are worn as charms. Some are naturalistic, but among them the eye-in-hand — a hand with an eyeball in the palm — stands out. It may be carved of cow bone or cast in metal, with an engraved eye in the palm or a cabochon-cut stone standing in for the eye. In Turkey, where blue eye-charms are favoured, glass-blowers make life-size eye-in-hand charms. Being quite large and fragile, these apotropaic objects are not worn as jewelry, but are hung on the wall or in a window for magical protection.

The eye-in-hand also appears with ambiguous symbolic content among the small artifacts associated with ancient cultures which may or may not have had the evil eye belief, such as the Mississippian tribes of North America. Some archæologists have theorized that the presence of the eye-in-hand motif in North America is evidence of pre-Columbian contact with Middle Eastern sailors; others have termed it an "intriguing coincidence" and left it at that. Eye-in-hand ornaments and jewelry have been found throughout the range of the archaic Mound-Builder culture, and they are strikingly reminiscent of similar protective amulets from Isræl and India.

HAMSA OR HAMESH HAND AMULET

The hamsa hand (Arabic) or hamesh hand (Hebrew) is a two-thumbed, bilaterally symmetrical hand. Hamsa and hamesh mean "five" and refer to the digits on the hand. An alternative Jewish name is the Hand of Miriam, in reference to the sister of Moses and Aaron, and an alternative Islamic name is the Hand of Fatima, in reference to the daughter of Muhammad, but there is archæological evidence to suggest that this downward-pointing hand predates both Judaism and Islam and is associated with ancient Middle Eastern goddesses whose hands (or vulvas) ward off the evil eye.

The hamsa may be made of metal or any blue material and it may be embossed or inscribed with vining tendrils, paired images of fishes, blue flowers, or a salamander. Some contain the Hebrew letter *ch'ai*, which stands for *"chaim"* ("life"), while others bear the six-pointed *Mogen David*, the Shield or Star of David. Some merge into the eye-in-hand design and feature an eye in the center. Although most hamsas are worn as jewelry or on key rings, in Isræl one can find large ceramic or enameled metal wall plaque hamsas bearing a Hebrew prayer in the center of the palm. Life-size hamsa wall plaques of turquoise-glazed faience are a speciality in Egypt.

BEAN, SEED, AND PLANT CURIOS

OJO DE VENADO OR DEER'S EYE CHARM
The *Ojo de Venado* or Deer's Eye is a Mexican charm against the evil eye. The dark brown seed of *Mucuna pruriens* or *M. prurita*, in English called Velvet Bean or Cowhage, its shape is that of an eye. Typically, it is strung on red string or a red and black beaded bracelet, and finished off with a plump red wool tassel. A holy Catholic saint print is glued on one side.

JUMBIE BEAN CURIO
In Trinidad and Tobago, *Abrus pecatoria*, the toxic red and black seeds known as Jumbie Beads, Rosary Peas, or Lady Bug Beans, are fashioned into jewelry that wards off *maljo* and evil spirits.

BLACK-EYED PEAS
Africans, African-Americans, and Sephardic Jews eat Black-Eyed Peas, *Vigna unguiculata*, at least once a year for good luck and to ward off evil.

AJVAN (CARUM COPTICUM) OR FENNEL SEEDS IN A BAG
Ajvan, also known as Ajwain, Ajowan Caraway, Carom, or *Carum copticum* is an herb related to Caraway, Cumin, and Fennel. In India, its tiny eye-shaped fruits are tied in a cloth or small bag and hung from the neck to ward off the evil eye. European Jews do the same with Fennel.

BALM OF GILEAD BUD CURIO
The Balm of Gilead, a small, eye-shaped Poplar bud, is valued as a charm against the evil eye in African-American conjure. A pair of these buds in a mojo hand fosters love and protects lovers from jealousy.

RUE CURIO AND THE SILVER CIMARUTA AMULET
In Naples a piece of the Rue plant, which has eye-shaped fruits, may be pinned to the clothes. Additionally, a silver talisman made to vaguely resemble the plant, called a *cimaruta* ("sprig of Rue") is worn as a necklace.

A NECKLACE OF CLOVE BUDS
Sephardic and Mizhrahi Jews use a needle to string whole Clove buds on a thread by their "tails": this is worn as a protective necklace by children.

LEMONS TO AVERT THE EVIL EYE

Not only is the evil eye destroyed or rendered harmless by burning, there is also the symbolic blinding of evil eye. Lemons are used for this purpose. This is perhaps because the shape of a Lemon suggests an eye.

LEMONS ON A SHADOW, CUT IN HALF
In Pakistan the Muslims place a person who is thought to be suffering from evil eye in a position so that he will cast a shadow. Four Lemons are placed in a row upon the shadow. A sharp knife with a long blade is then used to strike a single blow that cuts all four into halves at once. The halves are then thrown to the four points of the compass, care being taken that the two halves of any one Lemon are not thrown in the same direction.

LEMON CUT APART WITH TURMERIC AND SOOT
In India a Lemon is cut into three pieces and each piece is rubbed with Turmeric powder and soot. The pieces are waved over the entire length of the person who is thought to be suffering from evil eye. They are then placed at the intersection of three roads — one piece on each road.

LEMONS STUCK ON SWORDS
In India Lemons are used in marriage ceremonies where, to avert the evil influence, they are stuck upon swords, thus blinding them.

PIERCED LEMON KEPT AS A HOUSE-CHARM
In Sicily and North Africa a Lemon pierced with nine horseshoe nails and wound about with red thread in a random pattern "to confuse the witches" is nailed up over the inside door lintel to keep off *jettatores,* who cannot enter under it. In Sindh and Karnataka, Lemons which have been pierced are either kept or buried in the house as protection amulets.

LEMON PIERCED BY NEEDLES OR THORNS
In India a Lemon is taken to represent the eye of the person who has inflicted the evil and in such cases it is pierced with thorns or needles, waved three times over the afflicted person and then thrown away. If it is definitely asserted that so-and-so has been the source of the influence the pierced Lemon is thrown over or on the roof of the suspected party.

GARLIC TO AVERT THE EVIL EYE

Garlic is effective against the evil eye because it is sharp and spicy and because its individual cloves look like eyes.

FIVE CLOVES OF GARLIC AS A CHARM
In Turkey, individual Garlic cloves are employed against the evil eye. Women make little red and blue crocheted bags with five compartments, evoking the protective five fingers of the hamsa hand; each compartment contains a clove of Garlic. A single clove of Garlic may be carried in the pocket or place between the cleavage of a new mother.

GARLIC AND BLUE BEADS AS A CHARM
In Bulgaria a piece of Garlic and a blue bead, pinned to the left side of a baby's shirt protects the child from birth until young adulthood. When babies are born, Garlic is placed under their pillows.

GARLIC, HORSESHOE, AND NAZAR BEAD BUNDLE
In Greece, if a home is under threat from the evil eye, a horseshoe, an entire head of Garlic and blue evil eye beads *(nazarlik boncuk)* are bundled together and hung outside the window of the house and where the eye of the person who casted the evil eye might see the bundle.

A BULSIKA OF GARLIC
Similar to a mojo is the *bulsika* ("little sack") of Turkish Jews, containing Garlic, salt, and a blue bead. A variant is made with Garlic, Rue, a blue bead, and an amulet bearing the holy name "Shaddai," folded into glittery paper.

GARLIC INVOKED IN SPEECH TO ANNUL THE EVIL EYE
To counter one's own inadvertently cast evil eye, Sephardic Jews say, *"Al ajo ke se le vaiga"* ("Let it go to the Garlic and be nullified").

WHERE TO HANG THE GARLIC TO AVERT THE EVIL EYE
Sicilians and Greeks hang Garlic at the entrance points to the house, such as doors and windows, to ward off the evil eye. Braided strings of Garlic are hung in the kitchen near the back door to repel the eye, and also for use in cooking.

RUE TO REPEL THE EVIL EYE

Rue, a relative of the Lemon, repels the evil eye. Do not confuse it with Esphand or Aspand, called Syrian Rue, on page 43, an unrelated plant that also averts or cures the evil eye. See also the Cimaruta charm on page 52.

RUE IN THE BEDDING OR CLOTHES

Sephardic Jews hold that Rue wards off the eye from newborns and new mothers if it is hung on the curtains of the bed, kept in the bed, on the pillow on which the baby's head rests, or pinned behind the ear of the new mother, Boys are particularly susceptible to the evil eye before their circumcision, so on that day, a sprig of Rue can be tucked into the child's clothing. If allowed to dry, it can be kept pinned to the clothing for a year. Rue and Rrosemary together can also be carried in the pockets to repel the eye.

GILDED RUE ON ALMOND PASTE

After a birth some Turkish Jews decorate marzipan or sweet almond paste with a sprig of Rue. Almond protects because it looks like an eye and yields a whitish "milk" which guards the breastmilk of nursing mothers. The Rue is moistened with saliva, which is protective against the evil eye, and pressed onto a paper of gold leaf, called *alvarak*. The gilded sprig is then placed on a dish of almond confections. The gilded Rue may later be pinned to the child or to the mother for protection. Like mirrors and other reflective surfaces, the glitter of the gold distracts the evil eye.

RUE, ONION, AND SPIKENARD AS CURIOS

Sir Francis Bacon (1561-1626) writing on the topic of envy, said, *"For preservation against incantations and evil enchantments I have found the following to be recommended: invocation of the goddess Nemesis; the good prayers of those who do not gaze with admiration on or bepraise others; the blessings of those who wish to inspire courage are valuable to keep off the evil eye; the carrying on the person certain natural articles, such as rue, certain roots, a wolf's tail, the skin of a hyena's forehead, the onion, which they say the devil respects because the ancients adored it equally with himself, and that herb with a strong smelling root known as Baccharis, Baccari, [or] Guanto di nostra signora ('Our Lady's Glove')."*
The last-named is Sspikenard (*Inula conizæ* or *Conyza squarrosa*).

SHOES TO WARD OFF THE EVIL EYE

The shoe has a vulva shape and thus it protects the vulnerable.

OLD SHOES FOR BUILDINGS, FIELDS, AND BEDROOMS
In India old shoes are hung on new buildings and in planted fields to avert the gaze of passersby. A shoe under the pillow keeps off nightmares.

OLD SHOES PROTECT FRESHLY THRESHED GRAIN
In India old shoes are put in the granary when threshing is done for it is thought that this will keep the grain from being contaminated by evil.

THE SIGN OF THE CURL-TOED SHOE
Chashm-e-Baddoor ("far be the evil eye") is an old Persian saying found in Northern India and Pakistan. When written out as a slogan in artwork, it is often paired with the image of a pair of embroidered Punjabi *jutti* shoes.

OLD SHOES FOR MILK COWS
In India, old shoes are cut up into small pieces and the pieces hung around the necks of cows to insure a ready supply of milk.

OLD SHOES AND TIN CANS
In England and America, old shoes protect newly married couples from the evil eye. When the couple departs on their honeymoon, friends hang old shoes and tin cans from the back of their vehicle. The clanging tins drive away demons and the shoes ward off the gaze of envious unmarried people.

A NAIL FROM THE LEFT SHOE OF A MAN
In India, a nail from the left shoe of a man picked up from a road is a significant protective find and is attached to the child's belt.

OLD SHOE WATER TO FRINK
In India, a shoe waved about a person afflicted by the evil eye will cure him and drinking water from an old shoe removes spirit possession.

OLD SHOES AS A NECKLACE
In India, shoes are hung around the neck of child whose illness has been caused by the evil eye; after the cure is effected, they are thrown away.

GENDERED CHARMS AGAINST THE EYE

Gendered charms are traditionally carried by people of one gender only, or make visual reference to sex organs or sexual union. In describing gendered charms, it is an error of some folklorists to consider "obscene" charms displaying visual reference to penis-in-vagina sex. Actually, such charms of sexual union reveal the moistening and life-sustaining role of a goddess or female religious figure whose vulva and vagina protect the vulnerable penis from shriveling up and drying out due to the evil eye. Likewise, charms which resemble female genitalia provide the life-sustaining amniotic fluid and blood of childbirth to newborns and infants.

THE BUCKLE OR GIRDLE OF ISIS
An ancient Egyptian charm that combines the protective colour red with the power of a mother goddess's blood is the so-called buckle of Isis or *tyet* amulet. In fact, this amulet, carved of red jasper, represents the tied and knotted menstrual pad of the goddess; it protects both nursing mothers (Isis is generally shown suckling her son Horus) and young babies. It is a charm used by women, although any devotee of Isis may wear one.

MARTENITSA BRACELETS
In Bulgaria, a national speciality is the Martenitsa or March First charm. The basic style is a plied red-and-white wool cord, long enough to tie as a bracelet, or else done up as a bow-knot to be worn pinned on the bodice. The ends are often finished with one white tassel or male yarn-doll, whose name is Pizho, and one red tassel or female yarn-doll whose name is Penda. Martenitsas are given as gifts on the First of March, and people may accumulate quite a few, after the manner of friendship bracelets. They are worn for the protection of Baba Marta ("Grandmother March") during the unsettled days of late winter. When the wearer sees the first flower, migrating bird, or flowering fruit tree, signifying the union of male and female and the safe return of Spring, the bracelets are removed and hung from the flowering tree branches or placed on the ground near flowering plants. Although few Bulgarians think of Martenitsas as "gendered," the red of Penda and the white of Pizho are plied together under the watchful protection of Baba Marta to guard male potency and female fertility and to protect newborn animals, birds, and fruits from the evil eye.

FASCINUS
The fascinus or fascinum, which shares an etymological root with the English word "fascination," was an ancient Roman ornament or pendant in the form of a winged human penis. It might be worn as jewelry, hung around the neck of a child to protect against the evil eye, or suspended above a baby boy's crib, to ward off the eye of envy.

HORSESHOE
The use of a horseshoe to represent a lunar crescent or vulva is as ancient as the horseshoe itself. Throughout Europe horseshoes are nailed to doors to prevent the evil eye from entering houses and barns. The horseshoe charm has also acquired a second function, to collect luck to the building, just as a horseshoe-magnet might attract iron filings or magnetic sand.

CORNO OR CORNICELLO
Corno ("horn") or *cornicello* ("little horn") is the name for an Italian amulet to protect the penis. I looks like a long, twisted animal horn, rather freeform in design, and is carved of blood coral. In America it is called "the Italian horn." Due to its phallic shape, it is usually only worn by males.

BRANCHED CORAL
A naturally branched red coral "twig" is worn forked ends down, as a gendered female complement to the penile *corno* charm. It may be made into a pin as well as a pendant and is usually worn by women and girls.

TRANSGENDERING GENDERED CHARMS
Says catherine: "Carved red coral amulets in the form of the *mano fico, mano cornuta,* and *corno* were everywhere in Italy when i travelled there as a child with my parents in 1957. Every town had a jewelry store that sold them and all the men seemed to be wearing them. I wanted one badly, but my mother explained that i could not have it, because only boys were given them and i would be breaking a cultural taboo. They were, as she explained to me, a specific charm against impotence. More recently, Italian-American women have taken to wearing 'male' amulets like the *corno,* but due to the near extinction of Mediterranean coral caused by water pollution and over-harvesting, the traditional charms are rare, and reproductions in red plastic, pewter, silver, gold, and twisted glass are used instead."

MOJO HANDS TO WARD OFF ENVY

TO PROTECT AGAINST THE EVIL EYE OF JEALOUSY
A matched pair of Balm of Gilead Buds, a matched pair of nails, and a pair of silver dimes combined in a bag is said to protect a married couple against jinxes, and to ward off the evil eye of jealousy.

HERB BAG FOR PROTECTION AGAINST THE EVIL EYE
Carry Rue, Aspand, and Cloves in a cloth bag or place it above the door to ward off the evil eye. Fennel, Caraway, or Anise seeds may be added.

STAR ANISE TO WARD OFF ENVY
Many folks carry a whole Star Anise pod in a conjure bag to ward off the evil eye or *mal occhio*. If an entire pod is too large for your bag, collect the shiny seeds from nine Star Anise pods and use them instead.

ANISE AS AN APOTROPAIC CHARM
A pinch of Anise seed knotted up in your handkerchief and carried in the pocket is a simple protective measure against the evil eye. Its strength is said to be increased if it is combined with other protective curios, such as Rue, Cat's Eye Shell, or Agrimony, thus fixing it up as a mojo hand.

STOP GOSSIP WITH ALUM AND NAMES IN A BAG
It was a cold, rainy day in March, 1939, when Rev. Hyatt set up his recorder at the Cooper Hotel in Waycross, Georgia, and met "Informant #1152," who shared this mojo: "Take alum, a piece about big as a dime, and pound it up and put it in a little sack, and write the name of the party that you think that's interfering and put the name in the sack with that and wear it in your pocket. That would eliminate that trouble. They couldn't hurt you." Just as alum puckers up the mouth, so will this charm bag keep the person named from gossiping about you or messing in your business.

CAT'S EYE SHELL AGAINST ENVY AND SLANDER
Carry a Cat's Eye shell in a red flannel bag with Rue and Slippery Elm for immunity from harmful tales told by covetous neighbours, back-biters on the job, and hidden enemies posing as friends.

SPIKES AND POINTS TO PIERCE THE EYE

ANIMAL CLAWS
In ancient times, the Moon goddess was invoked as a protectoress of babies, nursing mothers, and milk animals, so her lunar crescent became an apotropaic charm. Paired animal claws, especially those of Bears, may represent the crescent in jewelry.

THE TIGER CLAW OR TIGER CLAW TATTOO
Before the wholesale ecocide which resulted in wild Tigers becoming an endangered species, the claw of an Indian Tiger was considered a potent amulet to ward off the evil eye. Less destructively, the Tiger claw may be made of metal or the shape is tattooed on the face and arms.

PORCUPINE QUILL
In the Kanara region of India, pregnant women wear a quill of the Indian Crested Porcupine *(Hystrix indica)* in their hair for protection against the evil eye.when they go outdoors.

A KNIFE UNDER THE PILLOW
To protect a newborn child from the evil eye, Muslims may place a knife under his or her pillow, to figuratively pierce or cut the eye.

A KNIFE OR SCISSORS UNDER THE BED
African-American hoodoo practitioners place a Bible, open to Psalms 91 *("There shall be no evil befall thee ...")* under the bed and hold the page open with a knife or scissors to ensure safe sleep and avert the evil eye.

THE KEWDA SPIKE OR HAIR STICK
The Kewda or Fragrant Screw-Pine *(Pandanus odorifer)* of India has sawtooth leaves, and a single spike is worn in the hair by women to avert the evil eye. A jeweled hair stick through a hair bun will also do.

THE CAMELTHORN SPIKE
In Azerbaijan, hanging a branch of the sharply-needled Yavasa or Camelthorn shrub *(Alhagi camelorum)* at the entrance to a home protects from the eye and brings happiness to the household.

MISCELLANEOUS CHARMS

A DRISHTMANI NECKLACE
In India, when a child wears a specially constructed necklace to ward off *drishti* or the evil eye, it is called a *drishtmani*. Black and white is considered a good colour combination to avoid the evil eye, so the necklace may be made of black glass beads with white spots, which represent the eye, and thus reflect back the evil. The pendant on such a necklace may be any popular amulet of the region, made of gold, silver, ivory, iron, silver coins, Tiger teeth, amber, carnelian, or mother of pearl.

BLACK JET BEADS
In Trinidad and Tobago, especially among those of Hindu descent, protective bracelets of black jet beads are given to newborn children.

TIKKA OR BLACK DOT
Following Indian customs, among the Hindus in Trinidad and Tobago, a tikka or black dot is placed on the baby's forehead to distract the attention of the evil eye, especially if the child is thought to be pretty.

FIVE METALS
An amulet made of five different metals tied or strung on a piece of twine or sewed to a woollen armlet is found in India. It is tied to the child's arm with a piece of black thread on a Sunday or a Thursday.

BROKEN EARTHENWARE FOUND IN A CEMETERY
In India, pieces of broken earthenware which have been found in a cemetery are perforated and strung on a wool thread to keep off the eye.

MIRROR CHARMS
Among the Kalbeliya of India (the tribe from whom the European or "Bohemian" Romani descended), the mirroring back of the evil eye takes the form of ornate circular mirror charms which are crocheted, braided, and wrapped with beads, buttons, and tassles. In former times these were used as dangles on horse bridles; now they ornament the key rings of cars. The practice of crocheting hundreds of tiny mirrors into fancy cloth — especially wedding garment cloth — is also widespread in parts of India.

COPPER ANKLET WITH GARLIC AND TURMERIC ROOT
In parts of India a large ankle ring made of copper is worn and to it are tied one piece of Garlic and one piece of turmeric root.

LIZARD AND SALAMANDER CHARMS
In India, children wear gold amulets about their necks in the shape of a lizard. When they reach puberty, they may lay them aside. Likewise Moroccan and Algerian Jews decorate hamsa hands with a Salamander.

CHARMS FOR DONKEYS AND HORSES
In the days before automobiles, draft horses and donkeys that pulled cabs and wagons where people might see and admire them were protected from the evil eye by apotropaic charms. Locally popular amulets for draft animals include blue faience donkey beads (Iran), Kalbeliya mirror charms (India), a scrap of Wolf fur (Naples), bells (all of Europe), images of equestrian mermaids called Sirens (Naples), and ornamental horse brasses, often cast in the form of a lucky horseshoe (England).

ELEPHANT'S HAIR JEWELRY
Ornaments made of Elephant hair are considered efficacious in India and Africa. During the late 19th century an Englishman was reported to do a thriving business buying Elephant hair and using it to make floral designs, rings, bracelets, and pins for export to Britain as amulets. Mounted with gold fittings, these are now treasured keepsakes. As Elephants have become an endangered species, such charms are difficult to find.

THE HAIR OF A BEAR OR A WOLF
In past times, Indian mothers made certain that a few hairs from a bear were tied into the belt which her child wore. In the era before the cruel practice of keeping chained "dancing" Sloth-Bears was outlawed in India, wherever travelling performers were found, there too would you find people who covertly attempted to pluck a few hairs from the Bears. In Italy, the hair of a Wolf served the same purpose.

DRIED SHEEP INTESTINES
In India, a child may be given an armlet to wear made of the dried intestines of sheep to ward off the evil eye.

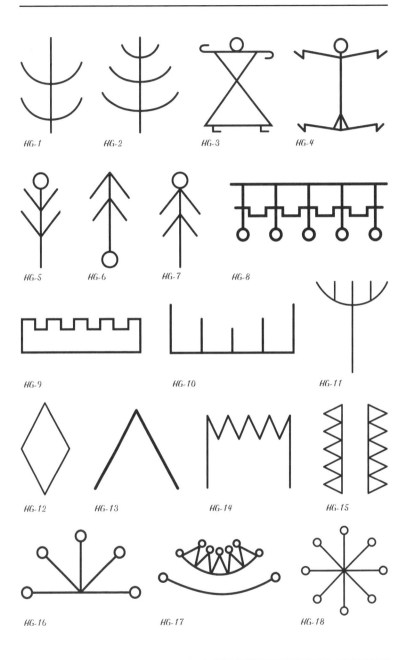

PROTECTION IN THE DECORATIVE ARTS

People are not the only objects of the influence of the evil eye. One's property and possessions can be equally harmed. Draft animals are protected from evil with amulets and by decorating their stables and harnesses. Rituals of various kinds protect fruit trees and standing or unharvested crops, and the harvested grain in the granary may also be handled in a certain way to avert any evil or contaminating influence.

Buildings are protected by painting them with the colour blue or by drawing, carving, painting, or glazing architectural tiles with apotraopaic designs, outside and inside, permanently or temporarily, upon the walls, ceilings, floors, and doorsteps, thus averting the evil eye on a large scale.

Similar designs are inscribed or glazed on pottery, and they are engraved or cast in gold, silver, copper, brass, and other metals that are incorporated into household goods, such as lamps, furniture, or tableware.

The designs are also woven, embroidered, or block-printed on cloth, incorporating ornamental protection as part of the clothing itself.

When used on fixed objects or as integral to clothing, apotropaic images such as these are seen as symbols rather than as amulets or charms.

This survey traces some of the most popular anti-evil-eye symbols found in the 19th century domestic arts of India, as described by the French Catholic missionary Abbé Jean-Antoine Dubois (1765-1848) in his book *"Hindu Manners, Customs, and Ceremonies,"* compiled and translated into English by Henry K. Beauchamp in 1897.

EYES AS DECORATIVE SYMBOLS

In India the eye itself is used as a neutralizing influence in averting the evil eye. It is thought that if one wears a representation of an eye, that it will either "outstare" or neutralize the evil glance of passersby. To protect crops, fruit trees, plants, and flowers, people fix an earthen pot upon a post in the garden, and on the pot a hideous face with prominent eyes is drawn with lime. Dragons and demons with protruding eyes and horns are installed in temples to avert the gaze of visitors. Sacred chariots used in religious processions, as well as modern trucks, are also decorated in this way.

On the island of Malta, stylized eyes or *ghajn* are painted on the prows of small *luzzu* fishing boats to protect the fishermen from storms and the boats from envy.

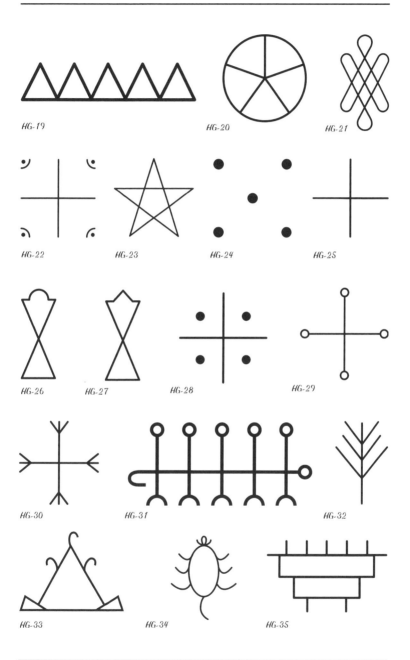

HANDS AS DECORATIVE SYMBOLS

The hand is one of the oldest human emblems found in prehistoric cave paintings. The hand and its fingers form an ancient symbol which is commonly used to avert the evil eye.

In the Middle East, the hand has been known to the Israelites as the Hand of Miriam, while in Muslim nations the Hand of Fatima appears in practically every home as a symbol of love, peace, and harmony.

The hand charm is found all through Africa, as well as in South America, where miniature hands of ebony, jet, or black glass are worn.

In the United States Native Americans used to imprint their mounts with the mark of the hand. The same sign is found in many places: in the Deep South; in the hills of Kentucky and Tennessee; in Lancaster County, Pennsylvania; in New York, Chicago, and other cities.

The hand is almost a universal symbol, perhaps because we work with our hands. They are important to us; they are our means of livelihood! They represent and embody our personal power, our mechanical ability, our art, our science, our agency. They are our means of defense. They convey our feelings, our gratitude, our approval, our disapproval; they caress, they fondle. The gentle touch of a mother consoles a child; the healer touches the sick; the priest gives a blessing. Yes, indeed, the hands are expressive and symbolic. No wonder they are used in so many ways by so many peoples as a protection amulet.

In India the hand symbol is widely used. For example, when a marriage feast has been completed, the women make an impression on the walls with their soiled, greasy hands. An impression of a hand is also made on the walls of the mother's room when an infant is born. Many also put the mark of the hand on the backs of their cattle.

When an Indian family moves into a new house for the first time, four rows of hand impressions are made on a wall. Five are made in one row; three in the row below; two in the third row, and a single impression in the bottom row. These eleven hands take the shape of an inverted triangle.

The Lingayats of India, after they have gathered the grain and as it lies on the threshing floor, make an impression of the hand in the grain. Many times they make an impression in the earth floor itself.

Muslims too have great faith in the power of the hand and believe it is a great protection. Your attention is directed to the two drawings represented as Figs. 1 and 2. These are symbolic drawings of hands.

HG-36

HG-37

HG-38

HG-39

HUMAN FIGURES AS DECORATIVE SYMBOLS

Another custom among Brahmins and non-Brahmins is as follows: On the fifth day following the birth of a child, certain figures are drawn on both sides of the door to the room in which the child was born. Figs. 3 and 4 are typical of what may be found, and represent human beings in caricature. They are also commonly found on pottery.

Figs. 5, 6, and 7 represent human figures, although not nearly as recognizably as Figs. 3 and 4. It is noteworthy to remark that the hands or arms are a predominant feature of these three figures.

Fig. 8 is also found on pottery. This is a refined version of Figs. 5, 6, and 7, and represents a series of human figures all holding hands.

FIVE FINGERS AND THE NUMBER FIVE AS SYMBOLS

In addition to symbols of the hand in design, it will be noted that the "five fingers" are the predominant features of Figs. 9, 10, and 11. These three designs may be found on doors, walls, pottery and even are tattooed or marked with henna on the face and body.

The spike of the Kewda or Kevada plant, used as a talisman, is also symbolically embroidered on the saris and head dresses of women in the form of a diamond or unfinished triangle, as shown in Figs. 12 and 13.

The spikey points of the backbone of a fish are similarly represented as in Figs. 14 and 15. It will be noted that in Fig. 14 there are five points, which correspond to the number of fingers on the hand. These designs are also embroidered and incorporated in clothing.

Other ways that the five fingers may be represented are shown in Figs. 16, 17, and 18. These particular figures may be branded on the hides of cattle to protect them. They are found drawn on the top and side pieces of the door frame and on the threshold of the house. They are found on the wheels of carts and vehicles and on the head of an ox-yoke. Shopkeepers put them on their iron safes, on their weights and scales, on their account books and on public motor cars or taxi cabs. Often when they venerate an image, these same designs are traced with grains of rice or rice mixed with Turmeric powder on the floor before the image.

Artisans do not always bother to complete the full design as in Figs. 16, 17, and 18. They merely draw or indicate the mystic five by five dots in a row. These dots have the same significance as the more elaborate figures indicated above.

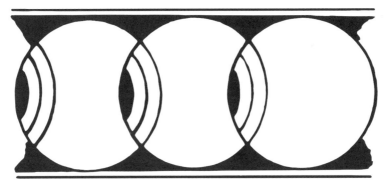
HG-40

HG-41

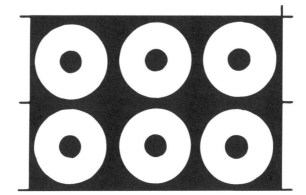
HG-42

REPETITIONS OF FIVE AS DECORATIVE SYMBOLS

A favourite henna mark which Indian women particularly favour for chasing away evil spirits is shown in Fig. 19.

As a symbol used in embroidery and as a henna design, Fig. 20 is very popular. It is but a simple circle with five radii and may represent a fruit divided into five segments, or the design made by compressing the tips of the fingers and the thumb into a tight cluster and viewing them straight on. Its resemblance to the five-compartmented, red-and-blue crocheted bag of Bulgarian women, which holds one tooth of Garlic in each sector, indicates a similar reliance on the number five to ward off the eye.

THE ENDLESS KNOT AS A DECORATIVE SYMBOL

Fig. 21 is an interesting design called the *srivatsa* or the endless knot. As one of the Ashtamangala or Eight Auspicious Symbols, it is associated with the teachings of the Buddha. In India, Tibet, and Mongolia it is drawn on the floors of newly constructed homes to protect them from the evil eye of visitors. It is also embroidered on cloth or engraved on jewelry.

EYE AND EYEBROW AS A DECORATIVE SYMBOL

Fig. 22 may be found as an architectural design, but it may also be engraved on a copper plate and carried in the pocket or around the neck as a talisman. It will be noted that the eye and the eyebrow motif is seen in each corner of the design.

STAR AND PENTAGRAM AS SYMBOLS

The pentagram, pentacle, or five-pointed star is a potent talisman against the evil eye and is often drawn, engraved, or embroidered on decorative articles. It must be made in one continuous line without lifting the pen from the material on which it is drawn. Fig. 23 shows how this is done.

The star is found in many places as a protection talisman or amulet. Sometimes it is a five pointed star, as in the case of Fig. 23; sometimes it is a six pointed star, as in the Star of David or Mogen David, which dates back to the early Isrælites.

The five spots, as they appear on dice, form another common symbol. In India these five spots may be embroidered on clothing with small seed pearls. In American hoodoo, a five-spot of oil or powder may be applied to magical items to fix or prepare them for use in conjure.

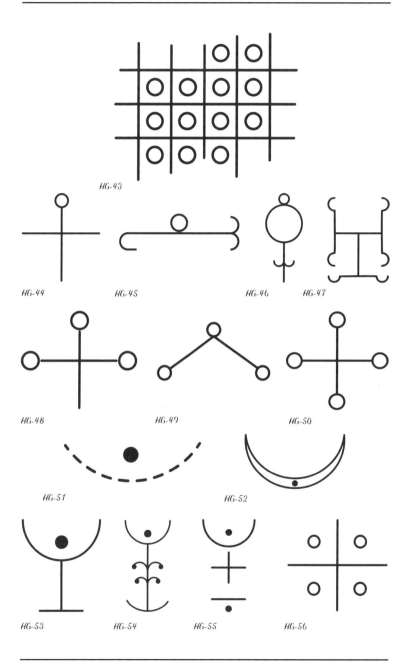

HEXAGRAMS AS DECORATIVE SYMBOLS

The six-pointed star comprised of two triangles is found in many cultures. The ancient Hebrews called it the Seal of Solomon, but by the medieval period, Solomon's Seal had become the pentacle, and the six-pointed star was called the Star or Shield of David *(Mogen David)*.

Whether the two triangles are interlaced or one laid atop the other, the meaning of this symbol is that the upward-pointing triangle is male or heavenly, while the downward-pointing triangle is female or earthly. The union of the two, as in the Martenitsa charm, provides power and protection for the reproductive systems of both men and women.

HEX SIGNS AS DECORATIVE SYMBOLS

In certain sections of Northeastern Pennsylvania as one rolls along the countryside in an automobile, one will see barns upon which are painted large stars within a circle. These are "hex signs" painted by the descendants of German settlers to protect the barn and its occupants from evil spirits. Here the word "hex" refers to *"hexerei"* (German for "sorcery" or "witchcraft"). Some of the stars are five-pointed pentagrams, some are six-pointed hexagrams, and some have eight, twelve, or sixteen points.

CROSSES AS DECORATIVE SYMBOLS

The Cross and variations of it are found extensively in India; it is not the exclusive property of Christians. Crosses are drawn on walls, baskets, and fans used in winnowing grains. They are drawn on the first pages of account books and embroidered on certain cloths used in the marriage ceremony. The cross and variations may be seen in Figs. 25 to 30 inclusive.

Figs. 28, 29, and 30 as well as Figs. 31 and 32 are frequently used as apotropaic henna marks against the evil eye. These are applied between the eyes. When marked, the girls are four or five years of age. Girls are never given elaborate henna on the hands until they reach puberty.

In the Karnataka region of India, Fig. 33 is commonly found. This represents the crown of a bridegroom and is suggestive of a five fingered hand.

Fig. 34 is a drawing of a scorpion which, with its feelers and stinger, make the number five on each side.

Fig. 35 is called the Hand of Shiva and its five digits recall the Muslim Hand of Fatima or Jewish Hand of Miriam, already mentioned.

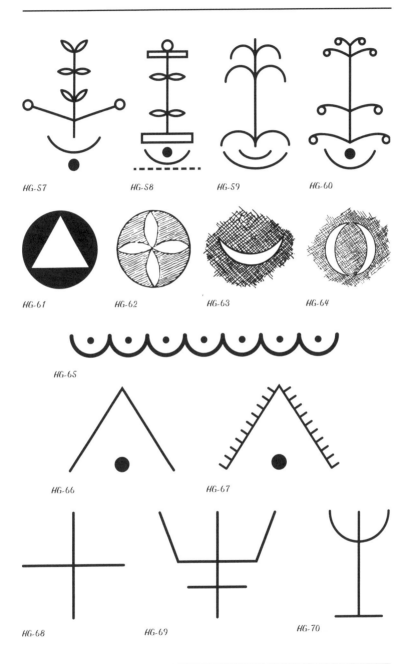

FACES AND EYES AS DECORATIVE SYMBOLS

Faces and eyes play an important part in the embroidery work of Hindu housewives, and the following figures are typical of the embroidery found on garments (Figs. 36 to 43 inclusive).

In Fig. 39 one does not see the face but only the representation of the eye. The same is true of Fig. 40 which is called "the eye of the bull." Figs. 41 and 42 represent the eye alone, while Fig. 43, which is called "The eye of the peacock," does not have the realism of the other designs.

CIRCLES AS DECORATIVE SYMBOLS

The circle is one of the most common conventional methods of representing the eye from its very shape. It is found as a part of all the figures shown from Fig. 44 to 60 inclusive.

In studying these various designs, it will be noted that in addition to small circles, there are many designs with little crescent-shaped "curlicues." These crescent-shaped marks represent "eyelids" and are common to most designs in addition to the circles or "eyes."

EYE HOLES IN BUILDINGS AS DECORATIVE SYMBOLS

We have previously mentioned that in many instances worshippers avert their eyes or cover their eyes while at prayer before an image or idol. This is done so as not to harm the image and so that the worshipper may not be harmed by the glance of the idol.

To carry out this theme still farther, one will find peep holes carved in the doors of temples, so that the visitor may look upon the idol without suffering harm. These peep-holes may take the forms shown in Figs. 61 to 64 inclusive.

EYES AND EYELIDS AS DECORATIVE SYMBOLS

In many embroidery designs we see Fig. 65. In this, the eye is represented by the dot and crescents represent the lower eyelid. This same design may be found as a decorative feature of flowerpots, baskets, etc.

Two variations of this which are commonly used as henna marks are Figs. 66 and 67. Here the dots represent the pupil of the eye and the triangles the upper eyelid. Note that in Fig. 67 even the eyelashes are figuratively represented.

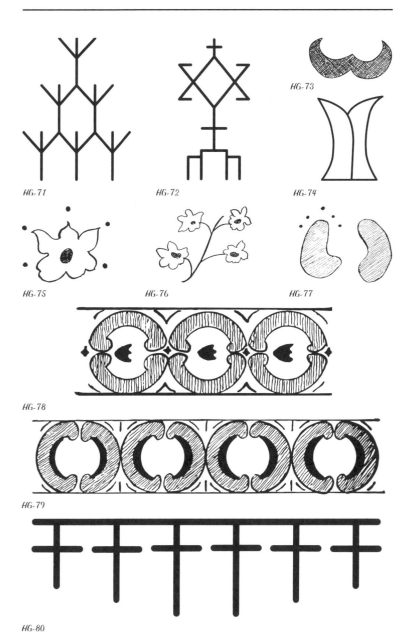

FEET AS DECORATIVE SYMBOLS

The foot is often used as a protective symbol to avert evil eye. If you have ever seen the footprints of birds in the snow or dust, you will at once recognize that Figs. 68 to 72 are "footprints of birds." These designs are used on pottery or engraved upon copper plates as amulets. The crescent Tiger's claw is considered potent, too, and Figs. 73 and 74 show two variations of this design.

The stylized footprint of a dog is often used, sometimes alone, as in Fig. 75, or repeated in a flower-like pattern, as in Fig. 76.

There is one design which is familiar to most of us in the Western hemisphere, for we often see it in Oriental rugs, in men's necktie patterns, in dress goods, etc. This is the design known as *godambi* — which Europeans call the "paisley." The actual Godambi is a fruit and it is shaped roughly like a Cashew nut, as shown in Fig. 77, but most artisans in India will tell you that the *godambi* does not represent a fruit or a nut, but is really an impression of a small foot.

As a matter of fact, in certain areas of India it is called "the footprint of the goddess Gauri" or "the footprint of the Moon." This symbol is common to both Hindu and Islamic art. Muslims draw the figure on walls with the back of their closed fist, which has first been dipped in lime. Hindus draw the design in their yards or plant flowers in beds of that shape. Farmers draw it alongside the doors of their homes.

Figs. 78 and 79 show the manner in which the *godambi* is worked out in sequence to form a decorative border design.

SEEDS AND PLANTS AS DECORATIVE SYMBOLS

Seeds are considered to have inherent powers to avert the evil eye, perhaps because they grow into plants and trees with God-given power. For that reason, Indians carry seeds, nuts, or herbs of various kinds to offset the evil eye. In the absence of the seeds themselves, designs to symbolically represent them will do. Fig. 80 consists of a series of simple crosses which represent Sesamum, while Fig. 81 represents a series of seeds. In Fig. 82 we see a motif which signifies grasses.

In Figs. 83 and 84 we see two kinds of plant symbols, both of which are used as tattoo or henna marks and as embroidery designs.

Fig. 85 is a representation of a Mango sprout, while Fig. 86 represents Pepper buds. A petal design is represented by Fig. 87.

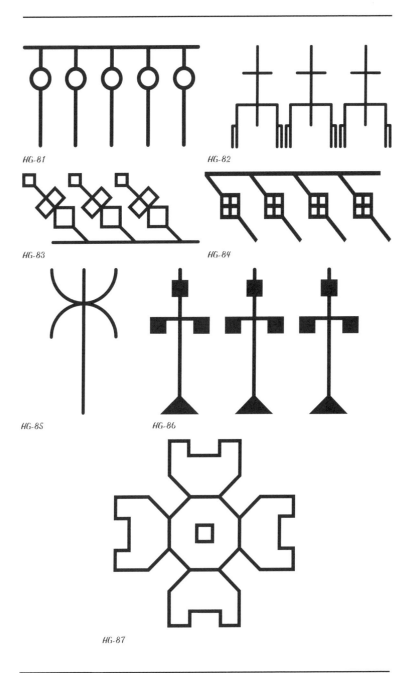

5. DIAGNOSING THE EVIL EYE

Sometimes the evil eye is diagnosed from the evident circumstances: The child was well in the morning, was praised or gazed upon, and began sweating or vomiting. The cause is clear and the cure can begin. But other times the diagnosis and the cure are linked together in a complex series of rituals, which vary by culture.

Water, oil, spittle, and melted wax, all of them liquids, may play a part in the diagnosis, or the ritual of discovery may center on an eye-shaped and liquid-filled natural object, the egg.

INDIA: THE FIRST GLANCE IN THE MORNING

In India, the morning hours are thought to be more dangerous, for a person or animal's first glance of the day is said to be the strongest. Later glances are less and less powerful, thus less dangerous. If the sickness came on early in the day, the cause is more likely to be an evil glance than if it occured late in the afternoon.

MEXICO: EXAMINATION OF AN UNCOOKED EGG

In Mexico, both diagnosis and cure are often accomplished with whole uncooked hen's eggs. If a child is thought to have been given the evil eye, an egg is rolled across the child's body or placed beneath the bed while he sleeps. When the child awakens, the egg is cracked open. If it is "hard" or "looks like an eye" then the evil eye is diagnosed as the cause of the child's illness. Once a diagnosis is made, a second raw egg, rolled along the chid's spine and arms in the form of a cross, can bring about the cure. This is called the *limpia* or "cleansing."

ITALY: OLIVE OIL DRIPPED ON WATER

In Italy, diagnosis of the evil eye is made by slowly dripping olive oil into a basin of water, a drop at a time, while reciting secret prayers that have been passed along only among females in a family. If the drops run together in the form of an eye, the evil eye is the cause of the illness. If an eye does not form, the cause is something other than the evil eye. The cure consists of cleaning out the bowl and reciting prayers while dripping oil into the basin of water again and again — sometimes for hours — until a perfect array of oil forms that does not resemble an evil eye.

EASTERN EUROPE: CHARCOAL IN WATER

In Bulgaria and other regions of Eastern Europe, when it is suspected that someone has given a child the evil eye, a diagnosis is made by means of charcoal. Generally this is done by an older woman, who prays and then sets about dropping charcoal, coal, or burnt match heads into a pan of water. If the charcoal, coal, or burnt matches float, the child has been given the evil eye and magically curative measures will follow. If the coals sink, the child's illness has arisen from another cause and will be treated with a different form of curing.

UKRAINE: MELTED WAX IN WATER

In Ukraine, melted wax, either from a candle or poured from a small metal utensil, may be dripped slowly into a bowl of holy water from a church to diagnose spiritual diseases. If the wax splatters on contact with the holy water or sticks to the sides of the bowl, the patient is suffering from the evil eye and curative measures are undertaken. It the wax falls calmly into the holy water and does not react against it or create a mess along the sides of the bowl, the cause of the illness is deemed to be something other than the evil eye.

GREECE: HOLY WATER AND SPITTLE

In Greece, making an accusation of the evil eye is not socially acceptable. In order to avoid direct accusations of having caused such a calamity, and yet obtain an accurate diagnosis, a family member may stand outside the church when the supposed perpetrator attends and ask all who pass by to spit into a cup of holy water. Because no one person has been singled out, the rite embarrasses no one. The holy water in the cup cancels out the evil eye and it is then taken home for the child to drink as a cure. The cure is thus the proof of the diagnosis, for if no cure occurs, the perpetrator has not yet been located or no evil eye was cast.

INDIA: ALUM IN A FIRE

In India, if a person is in ailing health and suspects that he is the victim of the evil eye, he tries to find the source of the influence by waving a little alum around himself. Then he throws it in the fire where it is supposed to assume the likeness of the person or animal that inflicted the evil. With this knowledge it is possible to lessen the effects or undertake a cure.

INDIA: CROSSROADS DIRT, BROOM, SALT, CHILIS

Another Indian test is to sprinkle a little earth, which has been taken from a crossroads, into a saucer which has previously been filled with water. A small pot is then obtained and into it are placed a few fibres taken from a broom, a pinch of salt, and a few Chilies. This pot is waved around the sick person and then turned upside-down in the saucer. If an evil eye is the cause of the sickness the pot will stick to the saucer for a full hour. This ritual is practiced in silence and with great solemnity. It is worth noting that this method of diagnosis utilizes a similar array of ingredients to the curing ceremony practiced by East Indians in Trididad and Tobago, which is called the *jharay*.

INDIA: ROCK SALT IN WATER

A Hindu test for the evil eye is to take three pieces of rock salt, wave them around the head of the sick person, and throw them into a pot of water. If the evil eye is present, the rock salt will not dissolve. How effective this ritual is hard to guess, for we all know that common salt will dissolve in water. Just as the above diagnosis resembles the *jharay* cure of the East Indians of Trinidad, so this Indian diagnostic method resembles the simplified Trinidadian *jharay* cure with salt.

INDIA: THREAD AND STONE

The Hindus of India take a circular stone and to it attach several black threads. This is waved around the person thought to be sick from the evil eye. Then it is thrown into a fire. If the sick man is suffering from the evil eye the thread will not burn. If it does burn, only natural causes are at fault.

PAKISTAN: THREAD AND STONE WITH SCRIPTURES

Among the Muslims in Sindh, Pakistan, a specific regional custom has been established to determine whether or not someone has been stricken by the evil eye. A little piece of thread is taken and wound around a stone. Certain verses or surahs of the Quran are recited over it and then it is thrown into fire by someone who has been positively eliminated as being a suspect. If the evil eye is present, the thread around the stone will not burn so long as it is attached to the stone. If this occurs, the thread is then removed, cut into three pieces and burned separately to do away with the eye.

INDIA: RELAPSE OF ILLNESS

In India, if one has been ill and goes out too soon and has a relapse, it is said that the patient has exposed himself to the evil eye and that he did not have sufficient strength to avert the influence.

ASHKENAZI JEWS: SOMEONE PRAISED THE CHILD

As mentioned earlier, among Askenazi Jews, the diagnosis of the evil eye often is made by an assessment of the circumstances that led to the sickness rather than by pure divination. For instance, a mother takes her little toddler to town and someone sees the child and says, "Oh, how pretty she looks! She is just adorable."

The admiring person may gaze overlong at the child, and if the mother does not take an immediate pre-emptive step — spitting onto the child, rubbing dirt on the child and denying before God that the baby is attractive, or asking the person who praised the child to touch her or spit on her — the evil eye then begins to operate.

By the time the mother and child get home, the child is sick to her stomach and crying. She is flushed, sweaty, and may have diarrhœa. Soon she becomes dehydrated and may be very ill indeed. The mother takes her to a conventional doctor, but "nothing can be done." She finally calls in a local healer — usually an older woman — who diagnoses the true cause of the problem as the evil eye.

In this way the mother soon learns to diagnose — or better yet, to prevent — the incursions of the evil eye.

AMERICA: CONSULTING A READER

Every day, African-American practitioners of hoodoo consult with psychic readers to see if they have been blocked, crossed, tricked, thrown for, hoodooed, had roots set on them, or been given the jinx or the whammy. Readers respond to these queries in a number of ways, including intuitive or clairvoyant knowledge, card-reading, pendulum divination, or photo-psychometry.

Tarot cards that show the evil eye is at work include The Devil (evil) and the Seven of Wands (envious attack from below). Both the Hanged Man and The Eight of Swords indicate a binding or tying spell. The Nine of Swords tells of a spell involving nightmares and insomnia, while both the Five of Wands and the Ten of Swords point to multiple enemies.

6. CURING THE EVIL EYE

The Hindus often say that no cure can render the evil eye permanently harmless and so they are satisfied if they can but reduce the effects of the glance. Other cultures speak of dramatic, almost instantaneous cures.

THE LIMPIA OR EGG CURE

The *limpia* (Latin and Spanish for "clean") is made by rolling a whole fresh egg over the victim to absorb the evil eye. How practitioners dispose of the "dirty" egg varies in different cultures. These are common options:

- Break the egg in a dark, shadowed place, unseen, and leave it there.
- Break the egg into the bushes or against the base of a strong tree.
- Break the egg and use it to draw a cross on the victim's forehead.
- Break the egg and leave it in a dish beneath the victim's bed overnight.
- Break the egg into a glass of water, set it under the victims's bed, and next morning read the shapes formed by the white to assess the cure.

RED WOOL YARN AS A CURE

Eed yarn or thread is used to prevent the eye in many cultures, but in New England it is not uncommon when a child has a nosebleed to tie a piece of red wool yarn around his or her neck to "draw back the blood." Those who do this may not mention the evil eye, but they do practice this cure, which is most certainly a survival from some earlier era.

AGRIMONY REVERSES CURSES

It is a common belief among hoodoo root doctors that one herb, Agrimony, has the power to reverse a curse once it has been cast. Therefore carrying Agrimony will reverse the whammy back to the sender.

DOUBLE-ACTION AND REVERSING ON A MIRROR

African-American rootworkers cut the red tip off of a half red and half black double-action candle, turn the candle upside-down to "butt the light," and carve a new tip on the black end. The candle is then dressed with Reversing Oil and burned upside-down on a mirror, surrounded by a ring of Crab shell powder to reverse the curse back to the one who cast it. The mirror reflects back the eye, and "Crabs walk backward" to undo the evil.

WATER OR HOLY WATER AS A CURE

GREECE: HOLY WATER AS A CURE
Holy water from a church is given to the child to drink and may be used to draw a cross on the child. If the remorseful perpetrator can be made to spit into the water before the child drinks it, so much the better. The holy water ritual of Greece is also found in parts of Mexico.

UKRAINE: THE WAX AND HOLY WATER CURE
In Ukraine, after a diagnosis is made by dripping wax into holy water, secret prayers known only to women are recited and the holy water into which the diagnostic wax was dripped is strained and used to bathe the victim. The wax is reheated and when it is poured into the water, it sinks to the bottom in a lump, indicating that a cure has taken place.

JEWS: CAST YOUR SINS TO THE FISHES
Many Jews perform the ritual of *tashlich* ("casting off") to discard the old year's sins by throwing breadcrumbs or pebbles into running water on the afternoon of Rosh Hashanah, the Jewish New Year. The Talmud recommends that the body of water chosen should have fish in it because "fish are unaffected by the evil eye" and one's sins will not harm them.

ROMANI AND BULGARIANS: DRINKING COAL WATER
Among the Bulgarians and the Romani of Bulgaria, if the evil eye has been diagnosed with coal or burnt matches in water, the coal-water may be poured on the ground or it may be given to the victim to drink, as a cleansing draught. Drinking one mouthful of coal-water and pouring the rest on the ground is common.

ENGLAND: BOILING A WITCH BOTTLE AS A CURE
In Sussex, England, where the evil eye is considered a constant menace, there are many cures. One such method, according to the *Occult Review* of 1916, is to take three ounces of new pins and put them in a bottle filled with water. The bottle is tightly sealed; a fire is made; the door of the house is locked and bolted and at midnight the bottle is put on the fire. The name of the person thought to have caused a spell is called out. When the bottle explodes, as it most surely will, the evil power is broken.

THE "SHOWING" CURE FOR CHILDREN

The "showing" cures are unique to India and they are only used for children who have been given the evil eye. Most are done in silence or contain the instruction to not look back once the work is complete.

SHOWING COTTON IMAGES TO THE CHILD
Three images in human shape are made of raw Cotton fiber and shown to the child after spitting on them. The images are then hung up on an outdoor wall and burned from the bottom up.

SHOWING BREAD TO THE CHILD
Bread is spread with sweet oil, shown to the child in silence, and then placed on a public thoroughfare. Do not look back upon it as you leave.

SHOWING ASHES TO THE CHILD
A handful of ashes is taken from the hearth, then another and another. Each handful is shown to the child. No word is spoken. The three handfuls of ashes are taken out and thrown at a crossroads. The person returns and washes his feet, after which conversation may be resumed.

SHOWING FOOT-TRACK DIRT TO THE CHILD
Earth from beneath the feet of the one causing the evil eye is shown to the child and then thrown into a fire with the words: "Fire upon his eye."

SHOWING A LEFT SHOE TO THE CHILD
A left shoe is shown to the child, waved up and down over the child's head, and then smashed to the floor.

SHOWING RED AND BLACK WATER TO THE CHILD
A container filled with a mixture of red water, black water, boiled rice, and pieces of Lemon is shown to the child by waving it slowly three times before her face. The four fingers of the child's left hand and the four small toes of her left foot are then dipped into the water. After this, the liquid is forcibly thrown into a crossroads at sunset. If the container is an earthenware bowl, it may be broken into shards when thrown. In any case it is left there, and you should not look back as you return home.

BURNING THE EVIL EYE AS A CURE

People of many nations believe that fire can consume the power of the evil eye and so it is burned symbolically to accomplish this purpose.

AZERBAIJAN: BURNING BLACK CUMIN
The seeds of black cumin are protective when baked into bread, but some Azerbaijanis prefer to burn them with salt, repeating the phrase, "Let the one with the evil eye lose his own eye."

INDIA: BURNING ALUM
When alum is burned on charcoal it has a tendency to form bubbles and one belief is that the evil influences go into these bubbles before being consumed. If it is thought that a person has been injured by an evil glance, a little alum is burned and the smoke from it is inhaled by the patient who says: "Burn the evil." Often the residue of burnt powdered alum is smeared across the forehead and temples and on the legs of the victim as an antidote.

INDIA: BURNING FRANKINCENSE
Just as alum is burned on charcoal, so also are frankincense or olibanum tears. The incense smoke is inhaled by the patient and the container of smoking incense may be carried around the room as well.

INDIA: BURNING GUM AMMONIAC
The acrid brownish-yellow resin of Gum Ammoniac (*Dorema ammoniacum*, an Asian member of the Umbel family), is burned on charcoal and the smoke inhaled in much the same manner as Frankincense.

INDIA: BURNING AN IMAGE OF THE PATIENT
A rough likeness of the patient is made of cotton fibre or flour dough, circled around him three times, and then burned.

INDIA: BURNING CLOTH FROM THE PATIENT'S HOUSE
Cloth which has been taken from the patient's house or, if possible, belonging to the patient, is unravelled or torn thin, twisted to make a wick, dipped in vegetable oil, and burned as a wick in an open oil lamp morning and evening for three successive days.

INDIA: BURNING BROOM STRAWS, CHILIS, AND EARTH

Straw is taken from a broom, to which is added Chilis and wet earth. These are waved three times around the sick person, out of doors. The ground is spat upon three times and the articles are thrown into a fire.

TRINIDAD: JHARAY WITH BURNING OF INGREDIENTS

The East Indians of Trinidad and Tobago were brought to the Caribbean as indentured servants by the British during the 19th century. Many of these Indo-Trinidadians practice Hinduism and retain traditional South Asian customs, including the *jharay* ceremony to cure *maljo*, or *mal yeaux*, the evil eye.

The *jharay* ritual of Trinidad and Tobago, which is also practiced by East Indians in Guyana, is generally performed for the benefit of afflicted children by elders or pundits, who may be either men or women.

Five leaves are cut from a Coconut tree. The green parts are stripped away and the stiff stalk or cocoyea is retained. Brooms are made from cocoyea, so if no tree is convenient. five stalks can be taken from a cocoyea broom. The remaining ingredients are five Bird Peppers, which are small, hot Chilies; five cloves of Garlic, although some use only the skins of the five cloves or will substitute Onion skins if Garlic skins are not available; five whole Black Peppercorns; and five pinches of salt.

Notice that there are five each of five items. The smaller ingredients are wrapped in paper and passed over the child with five circular motions. The five cocoyea stalks are then passed over the child five times in the same way. A prayer, formerly recited in Hindi but now often in English, is spoken aloud five times while the items are circled. It calls upon the evil eye to return to the one who sent it. The salt is discarded by washing it away and the rest of the items are burned in a fire, after the manner still common in India. No one present, from the elders on down to the child, may look upon the burning items or the evil will return.

INDIA: BURNING THREE BLACK THREAD LAMP WICKS

A mother will take three lamp wicks made of black thread which have been soaked in sweet oil. She lights the wicks and in turn carries each of them to all four corners of the room. Others who are present say, *"What are you doing?"* and her reply is, *"Driving away the crying of the child."* Then she throws each wick on the floor and stamps it out.

INDIA: A KNOTTED THREAD AND BURNING RICE

At the birth of a child, a knotted thread is tied to the child and the beneficence of Agni, the god of Fire, is invoked by throwing whole grains of rice, called *aksat*, upon the fire. This invoked power or *shakti* averts the evil eye, it is claimed.

INDIA: BURNING NAIL PARINGS OR HAIR

Parings of the nails or hair clippings of the one who gave the eye are collected, or a piece of clothing of the evil-eyed person is secured, and burned. The smoke is inhaled while saying, *"May he die."* By this they mean, "May his evil spirit die." They actually would not wish death to another person, as this in itself would be enough to bring evil to them.

PAKISTAN: BURNING GRAINS OF PEPPER IN A POT

The Muslims of Sindh build a fire in a pot or earthen dish and place it on dirt collected from the shadow cast by the victim. Then seven grains of pepper are thrown upon the fire and burned.

PERSIA: BURNING ESPHAND OR SYRIAN RUE

In the area once covered by the Persian Empire, comprising modern-day Iran, Egypt, Turkey, and parts of Afghanistan and Pakistan, seeds of the plant called Aspand, Espand, or Esphand are heated on charcoal until they explode and burn, while an incantation is spoken. The smoke of the exploding seeds is circled around the head and its fragrance inhaled to avert the evil eye. The same ritual can also be used after the fact as a cure for the evil eye. In this case it may be repeated a few times, until the cure is effected and the victim shows no more symptoms.

SEPHARDIC JEWS: BURNING WHOLE CLOVES

A ritual cure called *klavos a la lumbre* ("Cloves in the fire"), is found in several variations among the Sephardic Jews of Greece and Turkey. An odd number of whole Cloves, such as 5 or 13, with complete buds at their tips, are circled over the victim's head. They may be pinned together on a safety pin or left loose, according to family custom. After this, they are set on hot ashes or in a metal spoon over coals until they explode, and as they pop, a *prekante* or incantation is spoken:*"Here I remove from you all ojo malo, all evil speech, and the ayin hara, that you may not experience any evil."*

CUTTING THE EYE AS A CURE

INDIA: CUTTING THE SHADOW
Sometimes the ailing person will be asked, "Shall I cut your evil eye?" If he replies in the affirmative his shadow is "cut" seven times.

INDIA: KNIVES TO CUT THE FIRST GLANCE
Since the first glance of a person is considered the most dangerous, at a marriage ceremony, knives are left lying around to "catch the eye" of any dangerous person who joins the party.

TRANSFERRING THE EYE AS A CURE

TRANSFER OF THE EYE AS A LAST RESORT
It is a common belief that the evil eye may be transferred as well as destroyed, and when it cannot be destroyed, the only thing left to do is to transfer it to the ground and thus render it harmless to yourself.

TRANSFER TO THE GROUND
In India, by burying Lemons, pieces of broom straw, and baked rice which has been waved around a victim, it is possible to transfer the influence of the evil eye from the victim to the ground.

TRANSFER TO A MANTRIK AND THEN TO THE GROUND
Indian *mantriks* — spiritual workers who make their livelihood by helping clients with amulets, mantras, and spells — employ rituals and incantations to draw the evil eye from the patient and into themselves. They then free themselves of the evil by spitting upon the ground.

TRANSFER FROM COAL-WATER TO THE GROUND
In Eastern Europe, where the evil eye may be diagnosed and cured with lumps of coal or burnt matches in water, it is common to finish the rite by pouring some of the coal-water or match-water upon the ground, away from the home, to remove the remnants of evil. This practice is found among both Christians and Romani people in Bulgaria, Romania, and adjacent nations.

SALIVA AS A CURE

SALIVA AS PREVENTION, AVERSION, AND CURE
As we have seen, people of several cultures deploy saliva as a precaution against the evil eye or at the moment it is thought to be cast. Such preventions are not the same as a cure. In fact, they may be quite separate. The Jews, for instance, are well known for their licking and spitting, as well as their gestural mimicry of spitting, to keep *ayin hara* away, and they use these same techniques to quickly obviate the eye before sickness sets in. But once someone falls ill, they prefer to make their cures with salt water rather than saliva. The same is true of the Hindus and the East Indians of Trinidad and Tobago. So, despite the widespread tradition of using saliva as a first line of defense, there are relatively few examples in which it figures as a cure.

SALIVA IN ANCIENT ROME: CURING CHILDREN
Among the ancient Romans, children were thought to be particularly susceptible to the influence of the evil eye. As a matter of fact, the Romans had Cunina, who was the goddess of the cradle. It was she who was supposed to have the power to protect little children from the evil eye. The first century Etruscan-Roman poet Aulus Persius Flaccus wrote that old women were adept at averting the evil eye from infant children by applying saliva to the child's forehead and lips.

TRINIDAD AND TOBAGO: SALIVA TO FIX THE HAIR
In Trinidad and Tobago it is believed that rubbing your own saliva in your hair will cure the hair from any *maljo* or envious eye that may have been directed toward you due to your having attractive hair texture or length. The entire head of hair need not be wetted; instead, just the tips of the fingers are licked and then used to quickly brush back through the hair.

GREECE: DRINKING SALIVA IN HOLY WATER
When a child falls ill with the evil eye in Greece, a family member may stand outside the church with a glass of holy water, and ask the congregants to spit into the cup as they pass by. Holy water neutralizes disease, and the mingled spittle is given to the child to drink as a sort of "hair of the dog that bit him" cure.

SALIVA IN AFRICA: EASING BIRTH

In parts of Africa, if a woman in labour is having great difficulty in giving birth, the husband will admit that his wife had had a dispute with some man or woman and that ill feeling still exists between them. He spreads the word all through the village and all the married men and women come to the home of the suffering woman where they are required to stroke the body of the woman with the right hand, which has been moistened with saliva, a symbol of good health, peace, and good will.

If the woman still cannot bring her child to birth it is recognized that the one who has cast the evil eye is not one of those who has visited the sick woman but must be another, perhaps in a neighbouring village.

Suddenly the husband recalls such a person and he makes his way to the neighbouring village and to the home of the suspect party.

There he makes known his complaint and demands the party to revoke any enchantments against his wife by means of saliva. The one thus approached dares not refuse.

SALIVA IN AFRICA: EASING DEATH

In some parts of Africa, when a person is dying and the agony is prolonged, the relatives endeavour to trace the cause of it.

Usually it is found that the dying man has had a misunderstanding with someone and that the quarrel has not been patched up. Evil thoughts between them resulted in the evil eye having been cast.

In such cases the second party is sent for in haste and when he arrives at the home of the dying man there is not, as one might suppose, a reconciliation and words of regret as to the quarrel. The visitor simply passes his hand, moistened with saliva, over the chest or the back of the dying man. Then, it is believed, death will come quickly and easily.

Should the antagonistic person live at a distance and it is impossible for him to come quickly enough to the dying man, an apron or head covering with traces of his perspiration or saliva upon it will be sent along and placed upon the dying man immediately. This is assumed to be almost as efficacious as if a personal visit had been made.

To refuse an appeal such as this is unthinkable. No one would take such responsibility upon themselves. Even though two persons have quarrelled, the survivor certainly may not desire to wreak vengeance to such an extent as to cause hardship and suffering.

SALT AS A CURE

NORTH AFRICA: SALT IN THE DEVIL'S EYE
Among North African Arabs there is a cure for the evil eye which is aimed directly at mischievous devils or djinns. Arab women, when they cook a stew, throw a pinch of salt across the pot so that it will fly into the eyes of any hovering demons who might spoil the food.

ANCIENT ROME: DEALING WITH SPILLED SALT
Among the Romans, salt was sacred to the Lares and Penates and to spill salt was to insult these gods of the home. When a Roman spilled salt he would gather some and quickly throw it upon his breast thereby taking upon himself all responsibility and diverting all possible misfortune from his friends. Even today we acknowledge that spilled salt leads to a quarrel or to bad luck and we throw a little over our shoulders to avert an incident.

JAPAN: SALT IN THE WRESTLING RING
Japanese wrestlers sprinkle a little salt in the prize-ring to bring them luck before a match and to prevent being gazed upon with evil intent.

PENNSYLVANIA DUTCH: SALT AROUND THE COW
In Pennsylvania it is the custom to make a ring of salt around a sick cow which is thought to have been "hexed."

AMERICA: NEW SALT, NEW BREAD, AND A NEW BROOM
Many American housewives, before moving a stick of furniture into a new home, will first carry in a little salt and scatter it around. This comes from the custom of saluting the household gods of ancient Rome with salt. In some families, the old bread is finished before the move and the old broom is left behind. Then, on the way to the new home, a new broom, new bread, and new salt are acquired. The house is swept clean with the new broom, salt is sprinkled on a slice of bread, and that is the first meal eaten.

JEWS: SALT AND BREAD FOR THE NEWLYWEDS
It is a Jewish custom to give bread and salt to a newlywed couple to protect them against the evil eye.

TRINIDAD: SALT IN THE CORNERS AND OUT THE DOOR

In Trinidad people of East Indian descent ttake a handful of salt and pass it around the head of a child who has been afflicted by the evil eye. They then throw a pinch of salt in the corners of each room in the house and the remainder over the threshold and out of doors.

SIMPLIFIED JHARAY: SILENCE AND SALT

Among the East Indians of Trinidad and Tobago, the *jharay* ceremony consists of burning ingredients used to cure the evil eye. However, if a child is taken sick with colic or the evil eye at night, and all the shops are closed so the *jharay* ingredients can't be had, a simpler version of the ceremony can be performed using only salt. The person performing the ritual must silently and with no warning take a handful of salt in one hand and circle the child five times, praying aloud five times for the eye to be sent back, then immediately become silent again, and wash the salt away. No announcement that one is planning to *jharay* the child may be made, and no words other than the prayer may be spoken.

TRINIDAD AND TOBAGO: BATHING IN THE SEA

The East Indians of Trinidad and Tobago recommend bathing in the sea to remove the effects of the evil eye. This is essentially a salt cure, similar to others from India, but it also bears some similarity to the Jewish *tashlich* ("casting off") ritual held at the Jewish New Year or Rosh Hashanah.

JEWISH SALT-SEA-WATER CURE AT ROSH HASHANAH

The Jewish *tashlich* ("casting off") in which pebbles or breadcrumbs are tossed into running water at Rosh Hashanah, the Jewish New Year, can be done in any moving water, preferably that which is populated by fishes. However, if a person has the evil eye when the New Year arrives, the salty sea is best of all. The Sephardic Jews of Greece and Turkey take the afflicted person out in a small boat on the eve of Rosh Hashanah. Once away from shore, the person who will perform the cure recites a *prekante de ojo malo* ("ritual prayer for the evil eye") while holding salt in the right hand and circling it over the victim's head. The victim's face is then washed with ocean water and the salt is cast into the sea, with the words, *"Remove from him all suffering, all evil eye, all evil talk, all anguish of the heart, and cast it to the depth of the sea."*

7. IN CONCLUSION

To some readers it may seem strange, even amazing, that people of myriad cultures in distant lands or bygone times should believe in the evil eye. To them I say that these customs, traditions, and folklore are no more fantastic than many beliefs prevalent in your own neighbourhood today.

The truth is that many people who are surprised that there are cultures that carry a strong belief in the evil eye will yet retain and pass along their own culture's magical folklore without a second thought. The evil eye may appear exotic to them, while their belief in spell-casting, omens, miraculous cures, and the efficacy of amulets seems "normal" to them.

One man carries a raw potato in his hip pocket to relieve rheumatism; another carries a horse chestnut or buckeye for good health; still another burns a candle to make his dreams come true.

One will carry a Saint Christopher medal for safe travels, another a smooth, round stone he found upon the beach, "for luck."

One woman will avoid wearing opals because they are "bad luck;" another says that her "birthstone," the amethyst, brings her tranquility.

Many people "knock on wood" when expressing a hope or a wish, and say, "God forbid!" when speaking of the possibility of misfortune.

Some people believe that a horseshoe hung over the door brings luck to the home, while others avert their eyes when a hearse passes by.

Some burn frankincense to attain spiritual influence in the home while others burn Saffron powder or Pine resin to "cleanse a haunted house" or "remove crossed conditions."

These are not practices confined to an ancient epoch but actual customs which are practiced in America in this era of the atom bomb and jet-propelled planes. And it is not the ignorant or unschooled alone who follow such customs, for men and women of education are committed to magical practices as well. They may call it "superstition" and even joke about it to their friends, yet the feeling persists within, springing from some ancestral source, and they are spirit-guided to employ a traditional family remedy.

The evil eye, envenomed envy, witchcraft, superstition, hoodoo, hexing, the jinx, imagination, psychology — call it what you will — paranormal perception exists here in these United States as much as in any other part of the world, and as long as we know the meaning of a supernatural threat, we will seek and employ effective means to circumvent or overcome it.

8. ANNE FLEITMAN, THE WOMAN WHO WAS HENRI GAMACHE

A POSTSCRIPT BY CATHERINE YRONWODE

Henri Gamache, Lewis de Claremont, Mikhail Strabo, Godfrey Spencer, and the other pseudonymous authors who documented African-American rootwork in the 1930s and 40s, were widely accepted as cultural allies in the Black community. Their practical books on herb magic and spell-casting helped preserve older Southern traditions during the Great Northern Migration, between the two world wars.

The name Henri Gamache first appeared in print in 1940. Over the course of less than a decade this author produced six books on folk magic and spell-casting that were distributed through hoodoo drugstores, herb catalogues, and via ads in Black-owned newspapers and magazines.

As a young woman in the 1960s, i saw Gamache books for sale in every conjure, candle, and incense shop in America, from Oakland, California, to New Orleans, Louisiana. They were reprinted continually, and their copyright renewals were always kept up to date.

It took me sixty years to discover the truth, because the copyright renewers who reprinted the books falsely claimed that *they* were Henri Gamache, but in reality, this well-loved author was a Jewish woman named Anne Fleitman, born on January 4th, 1906. During her life she owned four different publishing houses, and one of them, Sheldon Publications, was named for her son, Sheldon Fleitman (1932-2011); her other son was Jules Fleitman (1926-1994). Under the pseudonym Sally Edwoods she kept an office at 6 West 28th Street in New York City, plus a ten acre parcel in rural New York which she leased to carnival operators. She died on October 24th, 1990, at the age of 84, and was buried in Mount Hebron Cemetery, Flushing, New York. By all accounts, she was a wild, fun-loving, politically liberal woman who strongly supported the Civil Rights Movement, so it brings me great pleasure to have recovered her name from obscurity and to have been the first to bring her story to the public.

Read more about Anne Fleitman and the Mysterious Mr. Young: LuckyMojo.com/young.html

THE BOOKS of "HENRI GAMACHE"
"Doorway to Your Success." 1940.
   Open Door Publishing Company, 312 Fifth Avenue, N.Y.C., N.Y.
"The Magic of Herbs." 1942.
   Power Thoughts Publishing Co., 24 East 21st Street, N.Y.C., N.Y.
"The Master Book of Candle Burning." 1942.
   Sheldon Publications, Highland Falls, N.Y.
"The Master Key to Occult Secrets." 1945.
   Doorway Publications, Astoria, Long Island, N.Y.
"Terrors of the Evil Eye Exposed." 1946.
   Raymond Publishing Corp., 116 West 27th Street, N.Y.C., N.Y.
"Mystery of the Long Lost 8th, 9th & 10th Books of Moses." 1948.
   Sheldon Publication, Highland Falls, N.Y.

Half-page ad for the first edition of *"Terrors of the Evil Eye Exposed;"* art by Charles M. Quinlan, 1946. Ads like this appeared in mail-order occult catalogues as well as African-American owned newspapers.

BIBLIOGRAPHY

ABBOTT, J., B.A, Indian Civil Service. *The Keys of Power.*
BEGUIN, Mme. E. *Journal Des Missions Evangeliques.* Société des Missions Évangéliques de Paris, 1826-1971; LXXV. I., 1927.
BEST, Elsdon. *The Maori.* The Polynesian Society, 1924.
CAPITOLINUS, Julius. *Clodius Albinus.*
DE LEON, Moses. *Zohar.*
DENNIS, Geoffrey W. *The Encyclopedia of Jewish Myth, Magic and Mysticism.* Llewellyn, 2016.
DRIBERG, Jack Herbert. *The Lango: A Nilotic Tribe of Uganda.* T.F. Unwin, Ltd., 1923.
DUBOIS, Abbé Jean-Antoine. *Hindu Manners, Customs, and Ceremonies.* Royal Asiatic Society, 1864.
DUNDES, Alan. *The Evil Eye: A Casebook.* University of Wisconsin Press, 1981.
EBELING, Erich. "Beschwörungen Gegen den Feind und den Bösen Blick aus dem Zweistromlande." *Archiv Orientální,* Vol. 17, No. 1, 1949.
ELLIOTT, J. H. *Beware the Evil Eye.* Cascade Books, 2015.
ELWORTHY, Frederick. *The Evil Eye.* John Murray, 1895, and many subsequent reprints.
FORTUNE, R. F. *Sorcerers of Dobu.* E. P. Dutton and Co., 1932.
FOWLER, W. Warde. "On the Toga Prætexta of Roman Children" *Classical Review*, X, 1896.
FRAZER. *The Fasti of Ovid*, Cambridge University Press, 1929.
"G. A. L. W." "Witches in Sussex," *Occult Review,* 1916.
HELIODORUS OF EMESA. *Æthiopica.*
HOBLEY, C. W. *Bantu Beliefs and Magic.* H. F. and G. Witherby, 1922.
IZAGUIRRE, Bernardino. *Historia de las Misiones Franciscanas en el Oriente del Peru,* Vol. I., Talleres Tipográficos de la Penitenciaría, 1922.
KENYON, Theda. *Witches Still Live.* Vail-Ballou Press., 1929.
KOTZÉ, Zacharias."The Evil Eye of Sumerian Deities." *Asian and African Studies,* Vol. 26, No. 1, 2017.
KUHLMAN, August C.H. *Berichte der Rheinischen Missionsgesellschaft. Barmen,* 1914.
LACTANTIUS. *Institutions.*
LÉVY, Isaac Jack and Zumwalt, Rosemary Lévy. *Ritual Lore of Sephardic Women.* University of Illinois Press. 2002.
LEVY-BRUHL, Lucien. *Primitive Mentality.* Allen and Unwin, 1923.
LEVY-BRUHL, Lucien. *Primitives and the Supernatural.* Allen and Unwin, 1935.
MOSES [attributed] et al. *The Holy Bible, Old and New Testaments* (King James Version).
OYLER, Rev. D. S. "The Shilluk's Belief in the Evil Eye." *Sudan Notes and Records,*1919.
PLUTARCH. *Romulus.*
SELIGMANN, Siegfried. *Der Böse Blick.* Barsdorf, 1910. Reprinted as *Die Zauberkraft des Auges und das Berufen.* De Gruyter, 1922.
SMITH, Edwin and Dale, Andrew. *The Ila-speaking Peoples of Northern Rhodesia.* Macmillan, 1920.
SUETONIUS. *Divus Julius.*
TERTULLIAN. *Ad Nationes.*
THOMSEN, Marie-Louise. "The Evil Eye in Mesopotamia." *Journal of Near Eastern Studies,* Volume 51, Number 1, University of Chicago Press, Jan. 1992.
TRACHTENBERG, Joshua. *Jewish Magic and Superstition.* Jewish Book House,1939.
[VARIOUS] "The Babylonian Talmud, edited by. Malinowitz and Schorr." Artscroll, 1984.
WEISS, Dr. Jeremy. *The Grimoire of Practical Jewish Magic for Everyone.* Dr. Jeremy Weiss, 2020.
WESTERMARCK, E. *Ritual and Belief in Morocco.* Macmillan and Co., Ltd., 1926.
WILDER, L. A. "Legal Status of Seers and Necromancers," *Case and Comment,* Nov., 1914.
YRONWODE, Catherine, and Gregory Lee White. *How to Use Amulets, Charms, and Talismans in the Hoodoo and Conjure Tradition.* Lucky Mojo, 2021.
YRONWODE, Catherine. "The Evil Eye." LuckyMojo.com/evileye.html
YRONWODE, Catherine. "The Lucky W Amulet Archive." AmuletArchive.com